Sherman Antitrust Act

Southern High Media Center
Harwood, MD 20776

LANDMARK LEGISLATION

Sherman
Antitrust Act

Richard Worth

mc **Marshall Cavendish**
Benchmark
New York

Library of Congress Cataloging-in-Publication Data

Worth, Richard.
Sherman Antitrust Act / by Richard Worth.
p. cm. -- (Landmark legislation)
Includes bibliographical references and index.
ISBN 978-1-60870-487-3 (Print) ISBN 978-1-60870-709-6 (eBook)
1. Antitrust law—United States—History—Juvenile literature. 2. United States. Sherman Act—Juvenile literature. I. Title.
KF1649.85.W67 2012
343.73'0721—dc22
2010023496

Publisher: Michelle Bisson
Art Director: Anahid Hamparian
Series Designer: Sonia Chaghatzbanian

Cover: In this 1884 political cartoon Standard Oil is portrayed as an octopus-like monopoly snapping up smaller oil companies, savings banks, railroads, the shipping industry, government, and businessmen in its vast tentacles.

Photo research by Custom Communications, Inc.
Cover photo: *Getty Images*
The photographs in this book are used by permission and through the courtesy of: *AP Wide World Photos*: AP Images: 13, 19, 63, 80, 89, 93, 106; AP/Pat Wellenbach: 2, 65; AP/PR Newswire: 83; AP/Tom Gannam: 100; *Library of Congress*: 3, 11, 21, 26, 43, 47, 49, 54, 55, 59; *National Archives and Records Administration*: 6; *North Wind Pictures Archives*: 10, 24, 32, 35, 37, 40; *Getty Images*: 68, 114; Getty/FPG: 52; Getty/Time & Life Pictures: 68, 77; Bettman/*Corbis*: 75.

Printed in Malaysia (T)
1 3 5 6 4 2

Contents

Congress of the United States of America;

At the First Session,

Begun and held at the City of Washington on Monday, the second day of December, one thousand eight hundred and eighty-nine.

AN ACT

To protect trade and commerce against unlawful restraints and monopolies.

Be it enacted by the Senate and House of Representatives of the United States of America in Congress assembled,

Sec. 1. Every contract, combination in the form of trust or otherwise, or conspiracy, in restraint of trade or commerce among the several States, or with foreign nations, is hereby declared to be illegal. Every person who shall make any such contract or engage in any such combination or conspiracy, shall be deemed guilty of a misdemeanor, and, on conviction thereof, shall be punished by fine not exceeding five thousand dollars, or by imprisonment not exceeding one year, or by both said punishments, in the discretion of the court.

Sec. 2. Every person who shall monopolize, or attempt to monopolize, or combine or conspire with any other person or persons, to monopolize any part of the trade or commerce among the several States, or with foreign nations, shall be deemed guilty of a misdemeanor, and, on conviction thereof, shall be punished by fine not exceeding five thousand dollars, or by imprisonment not exceeding one year, or by both said punishments, in the discretion of the court.

Sec. 3. Every contract, combination in form of trust or otherwise, or conspiracy, in restraint of trade or commerce in any Territory of the United States or of the District of Columbia, or in restraint of trade or commerce between any such Territory and another, or between any such Territory or Territories and any State or States or the District of Columbia, or with foreign nations, or between the District of Columbia and any State or States or foreign nations, is hereby declared illegal. Every person who shall make any such contract or engage in any such combination or conspiracy, shall be deemed guilty of a misdemeanor, and, on conviction thereof, shall be punished by fine not exceeding five thousand dollars, or by imprisonment not exceeding one year, or by both said punishments, in the discretion of the court.

Sec 4. The several circuit courts of the United States are hereby

A copy of the Sherman Act, passed in 1890. This antitrust legislation has changed the way companies do business ever since.

Reining in Monopoly Businesses

In 1890, the United States Congress passed the Sherman Antitrust Act.

This new legislation was designed to deal with giant monopolies, known as trusts, which threatened to dominate the American economy by controlling prices and driving out competition. During the first two decades after the Sherman Act was passed, a series of cases came to the Supreme Court that enabled the justices to interpret the meaning of the new antitrust legislation. In addition, Congress passed new laws, such as the Clayton Antitrust Act in 1914, spelling out the Sherman Act in more detail and giving more power to the federal government to investigate alleged antitrust violations. In 1911, the federal government won an important case against Standard Oil of New Jersey, breaking up a giant monopoly. In the 1920s, other cases were brought before the Supreme Court that involved price fixing, which was illegal under the Sherman Act.

Labor unions were a special case under the Sherman Act.

The Clayton Antitrust Act, as well as the Norris–La Guardia Act of 1932 and the National Labor Relations Act of 1935, stated that the Sherman Act did not outlaw union organizing activities. During the 1940s, the Supreme Court decided several cases that upheld the constitutionality of this new legislation. Over the next two decades, the Sherman Act was tested in cases involving professional sports, including Major League Baseball and the National Football League.

Legal cases often start in one of ninety-four U.S. District Courts, and then they may be appealed to one of thirteen U.S. Courts of Appeals, and finally appealed again to the U.S. Supreme Court. Between the 1970s and 1990s, the Supreme Court heard important antitrust cases involving franchising, boycotts, and mergers. In the twenty-first century, important cases focused on monopolies involving Microsoft.

CHAPTER ONE

The Trusts and the U.S. Congress

As he looked back over his success creating the Standard Oil Company—one of the world's most powerful organizations—John D. Rockefeller wrote: "The time was ripe for it. It had to come. . . . The day of combination is here to stay. *Individualism has gone,* never to return."

By "combination," Rockefeller was referring to large organizations that were made up of many smaller companies, and popularly known as trusts. These trusts, sometimes called monopolies, had taken control of entire areas of the U.S. economy, such as sugar, beef, and oil. A monopoly is an organization that controls at least 75 to 80 percent of the market. Standard Oil, for example, controlled 90 percent of the oil refining business by 1878. As a result of this monopoly, Standard Oil could set the price of oil, giving the company enormous power over the American economy. It was this power to drive out competition that finally prompted Congress to pass a new law against the trusts in 1890. Introduced

The building of railroads across the country, such as the New York Central and Hudson River Railroad, led to the industrialization of post-Civil War America.

by Senator John Sherman of Ohio, it was called the Sherman Antitrust Act.

THE INDUSTRIAL REVOLUTION

In the early nineteenth century, the United States experienced an industrial revolution. During that period, Americans built more factories and more railroads than any other nation in history. The success of this industrial revolution was due in part to vast deposits of raw materials. Large reserves of oil and coal in states such as Pennsylvania and West Virginia were available to power the factories. Iron ore mined in Wisconsin, Minnesota, and Michigan was available to build steam engines for railroads or to be turned into steel for miles of railroad tracks.

The industrial revolution also relied on the innovations of American inventors such as George Pullman, who manufactured sleeper cars for people who wanted to take overnight trips on railroad trains, and Alexander Graham Bell, who developed the telephone. Other inventors produced machines, such as the typewriter and the cash register, that revolutionized offices and stores. A major innovation came in the form of better agricultural equipment for harvesting crops and refrigeration cars that allowed railroads to transport food across the nation. Finally, there was an abundance of American workers to labor in the mines and factories. Many of them were immigrants who came from Europe seeking better wages and more opportunities in the United

In the late 1800s, European immigrants headed to the United States en masse. They formed a giant pool of ready labor for the new industries that arose, especially in manufacturing.

States. Between 1870 and 1900, the number of workers in manufacturing more than doubled to 7 million people.

Meanwhile, the U.S. Congress encouraged the growth of business. It passed high tariffs, or taxes, on products being imported from abroad, making them more expensive than manufactured items produced in the United States. This protected American industries, such as steel and railroads. Congress also did very little to stand in the way of men such as John D. Rockefeller who wanted to build monopolies in specific economic fields. Powerful trusts arose in sugar, controlled by Henry O. Havemeyer, and in tobacco, which was dominated by James Buchanan Duke, who organized the American Tobacco Company.

These men also had the power to finance political campaigns and influence the men that they helped elect to Congress. A political cartoon of the period showed a U.S. Senate dominated by the trusts. It stated: "This is a Senate of the Monopolists, by the Monopolists and for the Monopolists."

ROCKEFELLER AND STANDARD OIL

Among the most prominent examples of the monopolies was Rockefeller's Standard Oil. John D. Rockefeller was born in Richford, New York, in 1839. His father, William Avery "Big Bill" Rockefeller, was something of a con artist. According to Keith Poole, political scientist, "William Avery Rockefeller was a 'pitch man'—a 'Doctor' who claimed he could cure cancers and charged up to $25 a treatment. He was gone for months at a time traveling around the West from town to town [selling his fake cures] and would return to wherever the family was living with substantial sums of cash."

By 1853, the Rockefellers had moved to Strongsville, Ohio, outside of Cleveland, where John went to high school and

The Standard Oil Company, formed by John D. Rockefeller Sr., became synonymous in the public mind with monopoly. Indeed, Rockefeller was the first billionaire in the United States.

achieved high grades in math, not surprising because of his ability to do difficult arithmetic problems in his head. Rockefeller briefly attended college, where he learned bookkeeping and other business skills. Soon afterward, he went to work as an assistant bookkeeper at Hewitt and Tuttle, a merchant firm. In 1859, Rockefeller set up his own firm dealing in grain and hay, but he believed that the center of the grain trade lay farther west of Cleveland along the great prairies of the United States.

That same year, oil was discovered near Titusville, Pennsylvania. In the past, Americans had lit their lamps using oil from whales killed at sea. But by the 1850s, the supply of whales was declining, and the cost of whale oil had skyrocketed. Oil from underground could be refined into kerosene, which provided a cheap, bright, and clean source of lighting. Oil was also used as a lubricant for industrial machinery. Rockefeller believed that oil refining provided a great opportunity for anyone who went into the business.

Therefore, in 1863 he set up his own oil refining business—Andrews, Clark and Company—which competed with other oil companies in the Cleveland area. Along with many other entrepreneurs, he saw the future in oil. Rockefeller figured out how to run his company more efficiently than his competitors. According to Poole, Rockefeller built better refineries than his rivals. He also owned a barrel-making operation for transporting the oil, as well as boats for shipping it from the Great Lakes to the eastern seaboard. This attempt to place every aspect of the business under one management is called vertical integration. It would be the same as an automobile company that controlled the products—such as tires, glass, and steel—that went into making the cars.

By 1870, Rockefeller had established the Standard Oil Company, one of the leading oil refiners in the United States. Meanwhile he had also embarked on a strategy to drive his competitors out of business—a concept known as horizontal integration. This is an effort to control all competitors in the same industry, like an automobile company that takes over all the other car companies. According to historian Ron Chernow, author of *Titan: The Life of John D. Rockefeller, Sr.*, one method he used was dropping his prices so low that other refiners could not compete. He negotiated low shipping prices with railroads that transported some of his oil. Since Standard Oil could promise the railroads large shipments, they agreed to lower their shipping rates. Meanwhile, the railroads also made secret agreements with Rockefeller to charge higher rates to his smaller competitors, undercutting their profits.

By the early 1870s, he had driven almost all of his competitors around Cleveland out of business. Rockefeller bought up other refineries in different parts of the United States. "Later some owners who had been bought out complained to the press that they had been treated unfairly," wrote Poole. "The evidence is overwhelming that Standard's rivals were paid fair—even generous—prices for their property. . . ." Meanwhile, on the retail end, Rockefeller did not hesitate to put pressure on stores in towns across America to sell only his oil products. If they did not do as he asked, Standard opened its own stores to compete with these merchants and undercut their prices.

In 1882, all of the businesses owned by Standard were merged into the Standard Oil Trust. Samuel Dodd, a lawyer employed by Standard, had created the idea for a trust. Under a trust agreement, a board of trustees was established and controlled by Rockefeller. The trustees selected the chief executives of the other companies that Standard had purchased. All profits from these companies were sent to the trustees, who divided them up among the stockholders in the trust. The trust arrangement meant that all the companies worked together to monopolize their industry. Similar trust agreements existed in other industries, such as sugar, salt, mailing envelopes, tobacco, meatpacking, and farm machinery.

REACTIONS TO THE TRUSTS

Leading industrialists such as Rockefeller reaped huge profits from their operations. Indeed, Rockefeller himself became the first billionaire in the history of the United States. Standard also succeeded in reducing oil prices from 23.5¢ per gallon in 1870 to 7.5¢ in 1890. Rockefeller claimed that this was due to the vertical and horizontal integration by the trust. But critics charged that the price of crude oil had also declined as it became more plentiful. Nevertheless, some Americans admired successful businessmen such as Rockefeller or Andrew Carnegie—head of the company that later became U.S. Steel—who had risen from humble beginnings to become fabulously rich.

However, critics of the trusts and business tycoons believed that by monopolizing a particular industry, they were setting prices that often worked to the disadvantage of small businessmen and consumers. During the 1870s, farmers and small merchants had protested the lower shipping rates given to big businesses by the railroads. In Iowa, Minnesota, and Wisconsin, state legislatures passed laws establishing regulatory commissions to prevent railroads from continuing rate discrimination. This effort was spearheaded by farmers' organizations known as granges. They held social events, such as dances and picnics for farmers and their families, discussed agricultural issues, and elected members to the state legislatures in farm states. These legislators eventually passed laws known as Granger laws to regulate railroads. At an Illinois farmers' convention in 1873, a declaration stated that "all chartered monopolies, not regulated and controlled by law, have proved detrimental to the public prosperity. . . ."

Nevertheless, the U.S. Supreme Court stepped in to stop the legislation from having much effect. In 1886, the Court ruled in *Wabash, St. Louis & Pacific Railway Co.* v. *Illinois* that a state did not have the right to interfere with the business of any company—such as a railroad—that was involved in interstate commerce. Regulating interstate commerce (business carried on across state lines) according to Article 1, Section 8 of the U.S. Constitution, was the responsibility of Congress. The commerce clause reads, "The Congress shall have power . . . [t]o regulate commerce with foreign nations, and among the several states, and with the Indian tribes."

While efforts to control the trusts were temporarily halted, the protests against their practices did not stop. Beginning in the 1880s, a group of reporters called muckrakers (today they would be called investigative journalists) began to expose many of the problems in industrial America. Among the issues were child labor in factories, terrible slum conditions for poor, immigrant families living in America's cities, and the unchecked power of the trusts. In March 1881, journalist Henry Demarest Lloyd published an article in the *Atlantic* magazine titled "Story of a Great Monopoly." The article exposed the corrupt business practices of Standard Oil and it had an immediate impact on the American public.

Referring to Standard Oil, Lloyd wrote, "Their great business capacity would have insured the managers of the Standard success, but the means by which they achieved monopoly was by conspiracy with the railroads. . . . America has the proud satisfaction of having furnished the world with the greatest, wisest, and meanest monopoly known to history. . . . The common people, the nation, must take them in hand. . . . The nation is the engine of the people. They must use it for their industrial life. The States have failed. The United States must succeed, or the people will perish."

In a speech to the Illinois Bar Association—a group of lawyers and judges—in 1882, Judge John Jameson emphasized that trusts and monopolies posed a grave problem for the United States. He specifically mentioned the railroads and "monster business establishments, owned by private individuals, of which the Standard Oil Company is the best known type."

In 1885, the American Economic Association, a group of leading economists, discussed a proposal that stated, "While we recognize the necessity of individual initiative in industrial life, we hold that the doctrine of laissez-faire [no regulation] is unsafe in politics and unsound in morals. . . ." However, the proposal was defeated by a majority of the association's members.

Meanwhile, small political parties that were committed to ending the trusts began to form. Since 1884, the Anti-Monopoly party had opposed the trusts, and it was joined in 1887 by the Union Labor Party. As part of its party platform, the Union Labor Party stated: "The paramount issues to be solved in the interest of humanity are the abolition of . . . monopoly, and trusts, and we denounce the Democratic and Republican parties for creating and perpetuation these monstrous evils." However, the Union Labor Party received relatively few votes when it ran a candidate for U.S. president.

Democrats and Republicans did not want to seem out of

When oil was discovered in Texas at the turn of the century people knew that it would increase the fortunes of those who struck oil, but the automobile was so new that no one understood just how radical the discovery would be. In this field in Beaumont, Texas (1901), the wells were drilled so close together that one could jump from one to the next without touching ground.

step with the growing pressure among many voters to do something about the trusts. In 1887, Congress passed the Interstate Commerce Act. The new law was expected to regulate the trusts—especially the large railroads—but not try to destroy them. To carry out this task, the new law established the Interstate Commerce Commission (ICC). The ICC was supposed to regulate the shipping rates charged by railroads to make sure that they were just and reasonable. Rebates to

Senator

One of eleven children, John Sherman was born in 1823 in Lancaster, Ohio, to Mary Hoyt and Charles Robert Sherman, a judge of the Ohio Supreme Court. Early in his career, John Sherman was an engineer who built canals, but he switched professions and became a lawyer in 1844.

Moving to Cleveland, Ohio, in the 1850s, Sherman ran for Congress as a Republican and won a seat in the House of Representatives in 1854. He later became chairman of the powerful Ways and Means Committee, which controls the spending bills that are presented to the House of Representatives.

During the Civil War (1861–1865), in which his brother William Tecumseh Sherman served in the Union Army and after was appointed commanding general, John Sherman was elected Republican senator from Ohio. He later left the Senate for four years, from 1877 to 1881, to serve as secretary of the treasury under Republican President Rutherford B. Hayes.

During the 1880s, Sherman returned to the Senate and ran unsuccessfully for the Republican nomination for president. He continued to serve until 1897, when he was appointed secretary of state. He died three years later in 1900.

John Sherman

Republican John Sherman of Ohio sponsored the bill that came to bear his name.

large companies and price discrimination—charging lower prices to large versus small customers—were eliminated. But the ICC was given very little money to carry out its mission, which meant that it could not adequately send employees into the field to police the railroads.

Early in 1888, Congress began to debate an antitrust bill that was sponsored by Republican Senator John Sherman of Ohio. The basis of the new law was the constitutional right given to Congress to regulate interstate commerce. The large trusts, such as Standard Oil, were engaged in interstate commerce and so were subject to congressional regulation. During the debates in the Senate over the bill, Sherman acknowledged that the large corporations had helped the American economy by developing the railroads and expanding industry. But when they prevented competition, he said, they had far too much power. Any nation that "would not submit to an emperor . . . should not submit to an autocrat of trade," he said. Finally, Sherman pointed out that some states had already passed laws against the trusts, so it was the responsibility of Congress to take action to make a federal law.

Debate on the bill, which became known as the Sherman Antitrust Act, continued into 1890, when it was passed in the Senate by a vote of 51 to 1. The bill then went to the House of Representatives, where it passed unanimously. On July 2, 1890, Republican President Benjamin Harrison signed the bill into law. In Section I, the law stated: "Every contract, combination in the form of trust or otherwise, or conspiracy, in restraint of trade or commerce among the several States, or with foreign nations, is declared to be illegal." The phrase *restraint of trade* referred to practices by a powerful trust, such as fixing the price on a product—whether it be oil or shoes—so consumers had no choice but to pay it. Section II of the law stated that any person or company "who shall monopolize or attempt to monopolize," was guilty of violating the Sherman Act and would be punished by a fine, imprisonment for no more than three years, or both.

The law was not designed to prevent all monopolies. Any company that took control of an industry, such as steel, because no other company could manufacture the product as well was not considered to be in violation of the Sherman Antitrust Act. This was a monopoly that occurred based completely on the merit, efficiency, and quality of the company's products. It resulted from fair competition. What the law deemed illegal was a successful effort—or even an attempt—by a combination of companies, who got together to fix prices, restrict competition, or cut off supplies of raw materials to drive competitors out of an economic field. This was considered unfair under the Sherman Act and an attempt to undermine the fair competition that was the foundation of the American economy. (Competition frequently leads to lower prices and new, more efficient products, as companies compete for success in the marketplace.) Finally, the Sherman Act applied only to "combinations" or "contracts" between companies that had an impact on interstate commerce. Under the U.S. Constitution, Article I, Section 8, Congress had been given the right to regulate interstate commerce. Commerce completely inside a state was regulated by that state.

Over the next two decades, the Sherman Act would be clarified and tested by a number of legal challenges that came before the Supreme Court and the lower courts.

Swift's Premium
Buy It Whole

Swift's Little Cook

Boil the Shank

Broil or Fry the Center Slices

Without parboiling

Bake the Butt

Premium Ham Shank with Vegetables

Wash ham shank and boil about three hours slowly. Remove from water and cook in the water cabbage, turnips, carrots and onions, until tender. Reheat the ham and serve as a boiled dinner.

Premium Ham Shank with Spinach

Wash ham and spinach carefully. Boil ham slowly about two hours and add spinach. Boil rapidly for about thirty minutes. Serve separately and garnish spinach with hard-boiled egg.

Premium Ham Baked with Tomatoes and Onions

1 center slice of ham, 3/4 to one inch thick
3 medium sized tomatoes
3 medium sized onions

Lay ham in baking pan. Slice first the onions and then the tomatoes on top until thickly covered. Add one cup of water and bake one hour, basting frequently with juice in pan.

Premium Ham Baked with Apples

1 center slice ham, about 3/4 of an inch thick. Cut off the fat and put (fat) through grinder. Spread on ham and cover all with brown sugar. Core apples and season with sugar and spice, put in pan and add 1/2 cup water. Bake in a very slow oven about fifty minutes.

Creamed Premium Ham on Toast

2 tablespoonfuls butter   2 tablespoonfuls flour
1/4 teaspoonful salt   Pepper
1 1/2 cups chopped cooked ham (baked or boiled)
2 hard boiled eggs—sliced   1 cup milk

Melt butter and stir in flour without browning. Remove from fire and add milk and seasoning, stirring well. Return to fire and cook until creamy. Add ham and hard boiled eggs. Serve on toast.

Premium Ham Baked with Macaroni

1 cup of Macaroni broken in small pieces
1/2 cup of grated cheese   1 cup milk
1 cup chopped cooked ham (baked or boiled)
1 tablespoonful of chopped onion, salt and paprika

Boil macaroni in salted water until tender. Drain, rinse with cold water. Add grated cheese, milk, and season with salt and paprika. Fry onion in a little ham fat, add chopped ham. Mix well with macaroni, turn into well-buttered baking dish. Cover with bread crumbs and bake until brown.

Baked Premium Ham

Put a Ham butt in cold water, then boil slowly (one-half hour for each pound), changing the water when half done.

Remove the rind, and insert cloves in the soft fat, cover thickly with brown sugar. Place in a baking dish with water, and bake for one-half hour.

Swift & Company, U. S. A.

Swift and Company were quick to advertise their meats, but did not choose to air their price-fixing practices.

CHAPTER TWO

Enforcing the Law, 1890–1910

The passage of the Sherman Antitrust Act in 1890 was meant to bring an end to the giant trusts, or monopolies. However, skilled entrepreneurs, who had grown rich from their powerful businesses, had created these monopolies, and these men did not want to break them up just to satisfy the federal government.

Among these businessmen was Gustavus Franklin Swift, a man who had begun his career in 1853 at age fourteen working in his brother's Massachusetts butcher shop. Eventually he opened his own company, Hathaway and Swift, moving it to Buffalo, New York, and eventually to Chicago. This was the center of the meatpacking industry, and Swift established his slaughterhouses near the cattle stockyards. In the late 1870s, Swift developed the first successful refrigeration railroad car, enabling him to ship beef across the United States to any city at any time of year.

In 1885, he became president of Swift and Company, which

In 1906, Upton Sinclair would change forever the way the American public viewed the meat-packing industry with *The Jungle*, his novel about the inhumane conditions in the Chicago stockyards. The fact that the industry was run as a monopoly made those conditions easy to create.

controlled an estimated 60 percent of the fresh meat market. Together with smaller meatpackers, Swift created a meat trust. The trust used any means available to control livestock prices. For instance, the trust sent representatives from its different packers to a cattle auction, and they worked together to keep prices bid on the cattle as low as possible. Then they shipped the cattle to the Swift slaughterhouses, raised the price of slaughtered beef that was shipped to eastern cities, and so made hefty profits. This was an example of price fixing. Swift was controlling prices across an entire industry—from the prices paid for live cattle to the prices charged for slaughtered beef. Swift and Company also received rebates from the railroads, keeping its shipping prices lower than the prices charged to its competitors.

Enforcing the Sherman Antitrust Act against organizations like Swift and Company was the responsibility of the U.S. attorney general, William H. H. Miller, who represented the federal government. Unfortunately, his office was both understaffed and underfunded. There were only eighteen lawyers in the attorney general's office in 1890. One of their responsibilities was presenting cases to the Supreme Court on behalf of the U.S. government, and the number of cases had tripled since 1880. In addition, there was very little money appropriated to investigate companies suspected of violating the antitrust law. At the state level, the attorney general was represented by district attorneys, who enforced the laws of the federal government. While the district attorneys were supposed to be under his control, they often operated independently. For example, Miller had ordered the district attorney in Ohio to investigate Standard Oil, but nothing happened because the local district attorney did not believe the case was important.

THE E. C. KNIGHT CASE

In 1892, Democrat Grover Cleveland was elected president of the United States. Cleveland appointed a new attorney general, Richard Olney. Cleveland had committed himself to regulating the power of the trusts. The Democrats had stated during the election that they believed in "the rigid enforcement of the laws made to prevent and control them [the trusts] . . ." to safeguard competition.

In 1895, Olney decided to bring a case against the sugar trust to the Supreme Court. During the early 1890s, a merger between E. C. Knight and the American Sugar Refining Company led to a near 100 percent monopoly on the refining of sugar, creating a sugar trust. The trust had bought from E. C. Knight four Philadelphia refineries that produced about one-third of the sugar in the United States. The federal government decided to stop E. C. Knight from making the sale to the trust, because the government believed it was a violation of the Sherman Antitrust Act.

In the American judicial system, cases like these were, and still are, tried in a lower court—a federal district court—before reaching the Supreme Court. After a decision is rendered in a lower court, it can be appealed to a court of appeals and finally, after a decision is rendered in the appeals court, appealed to the Supreme Court. But such a case does not originate in the Supreme Court. The Knight case was first tried in the U.S. District Court in Pennsylvania. There, Judge William Butler stated that E. C. Knight had not violated the Sherman Antitrust Act because the acquisition of its sugar refineries occurred within the state of Pennsylvania and did not involve interstate commerce.

The federal government appealed the decision, which eventually reached the Supreme Court. In 1895, Chief Justice Melville Fuller handed down the 8 to 1 decision for a majority of the Court in the case of *United States* v. *E. C. Knight Co.* Although Fuller stated that there was indeed a monopoly of manufacturing by the sugar trust, it did not involve interstate commerce and only impacted it "incidentally and indirectly." This meant that only an individual state could bring a lawsuit against a suspected monopoly in manufacturing that occurred within the state's boundaries.

TRANS-MISSOURI CASE

Meanwhile the interpretation of the Sherman Act was also about to be tested in a different case. Several railroads in the central part of the United States had been working together to set the same shipping rates. In the case of *United States* v. *Trans-Missouri Freight Association*, the federal government challenged the action of the railroads as an antitrust violation. When the case came before District Judge John Riner in 1893, he stated that the association had not violated antitrust law because it did not have a monopoly on shipping in the area that it served. Riner further stated that the association was not preventing competition, but it was stopping the type of price wars that often went on among railroads, putting some of them out of business and forcing many employees out of work. What's more, according to Riner, the association was not setting unreasonable, high rates, but reasonable shipping charges that were benefiting the general public.

The federal government appealed the decision to the Supreme Court. In 1897, the Court handed down a 5 to 4 decision for the government in *United States* v. *Trans-Missouri Freight Association*. Writing for the majority was Supreme Court Associate Justice Rufus Peckham. Peckham explained that the railroads were shipping freight across state boundaries, so their activities involved interstate commerce. He added, "The prohibitory provisions of the said Act [Sherman Antitrust Act] apply to all contracts in restraint of interstate or foreign trade or commerce without exception or

The Mood of the United States

During the 1890s, there was growing unrest among many people in the United States. In 1893, the nation suffered a severe economic downturn. Among farmers, prices for wheat, corn, and other agricultural products, which had been declining for the past decade, sank even lower. Meanwhile, manufactured equipment, such as plows, had been increasing in price. Manufacturers were protected by tariffs from companies outside the United States, allowing domestic firms to charge higher prices. Many farmers blamed the trusts that controlled manufacturing for this situation. The trusts contributed to the campaigns of elected representatives in Congress and had a powerful influence over them. As social activist Mary Elizabeth Lease put it, "It is no longer a government of the people, by the people, for the people, but a government of Wall Street, by Wall Street, and for Wall Street."

limitation; and are not confined to those in which the restraint is unreasonable."

The Supreme Court's decision in the case broadened the interpretation of the Sherman Antitrust Act by saying that no one could decide between a reasonable and an unreasonable restraint of trade. The association was restraining trade because it controlled a large amount of the shipping in its area and it was setting rates. Whether or not it had a complete monopoly or the rates were reasonable or unreasonable was not relevant, Peckham wrote. He added that the Sherman Antitrust Act prohibited all agreements in restraint of trade.

THE POPULIST MOVEMENT

During the early 1890s, farmers created a new political party, called the Populist Party, which was especially strong in the heavy agricultural areas of the South and West. In 1896, the Populists joined with the Democrats to try to elect the Democratic nominee, William Jennings Bryan, president of the United States. However, Bryan was considered too radical by a majority of voters. They voted instead for Republican William McKinley, who was elected president.

The rise of the Populists occurred at the same time as a group of reformers known as Progressives were pointing out the problems in America's cities. The Progressives included journalists who published articles in leading magazines about the plight of poor immigrants crowded into foul tenement buildings in city slums. At the state level, the Progressives led crusades that eventually convinced legislators to improve housing, build playgrounds for children in the slums, and improve health care for poor workers. One of the main targets of the Progressives was the giant trusts that were making a

In the late nineteenth century, immigrants, and migrants from the South, swelled the population of the northern cities and the coffers of the industrialists, while they lived packed together in unsanitary tenement buildings such as the one pictured here.

small group of people rich while the majority of Americans were struggling. The Progressives called for an end to the trusts and their control of elected officials. Progressives also wanted regulation of the railroads, better working conditions, and fairer pay for workers.

The rise of the Populists and the Progressives shone a spotlight on the problems that existed for many Americans. It was against this backdrop that the courts tried to interpret the Sherman Antitrust Act and deal with the power of the trusts. During the 1890s, a group of six iron pipe makers, who controlled about one-third of the market, had formed an association to fix prices. When a city or town needed to buy iron pipe for a water or sewer line, the job was put out to bids from various pipe companies. The association secretly decided which member company should get the job. This company bid the lowest price to do the job and the other members of the association bid slightly higher. By fixing the bids in this way, the association relied on corruption to control the price of the job.

The federal government sued the association for antitrust violations, and the case reached the lower courts in 1897. There the judge decided that since the association was involved in manufacturing and not directly in interstate commerce, the Sherman Antitrust Act did not apply. In addition, he said that the prices the association charged were not unreasonable and that customers were satisfied with them. The case was appealed to a higher court, the U.S. Court of Appeals for the Sixth Circuit, where Judge William Howard Taft, who later became president, wrote the majority opinion. Judge Taft disagreed with the lower court. He said that the pipes were being manufactured in one state and being transported for sale to towns and cities in other states, so interstate commerce *was* involved. What's more, whether or not the prices charged by the association were reasonable or unreasonable, it was still controlling prices and could begin charging unreasonable prices in the future.

This was an example of horizontal price fixing—controlling prices by many companies across the same industry—a practice that was illegal under the Sherman Act. Taft's decision was upheld when the case of *Addyston Pipe and Steel Co. v. United States* reached the Supreme Court. In an opinion written by Judge Peckham in 1899, the Court unanimously decided against the association. Peckham stated "The direct and immediate result of the combination was . . . necessarily a restraint upon interstate commerce in respect of articles manufactured by any of the parties to it to be transported beyond the State in which they were made."

THEODORE ROOSEVELT AND THE TRUSTS

In 1900, William McKinley ran for a second term as president. His running mate was Theodore Roosevelt, the Progressive governor of New York, who was nominated by the Republicans to be vice president. McKinley won a second term in office, but he was assassinated the following year by an extreme radical named Leon Czolgosz. At age forty-two, Roosevelt became the youngest president in American history.

The new president understood the opposition of the Progressives to the trusts and shared some of their feelings. As Roosevelt said in a speech delivered in 1902, "The great corporations which we have grown to speak of rather loosely as trusts are the creatures of the State, and the State not only has the right to control them, but it is in duty bound to control them wherever the need of such control is shown." While recognizing that big companies were here to stay,

William McKinley was elected to a second term as president in 1900, but in September 1901 he was assassinated at a public exhibition in Buffalo by Leon Czolgosz, an anarchist.

Roosevelt wanted to prevent them from engaging in illegal activities to maintain their positions in the market.

Roosevelt's speeches helped rouse the nation and persuade Congress to support legislation to control the trusts. This included legislation to create a Department of Commerce and Labor in 1903 to "monitor all aspects of industrial production." Congress also established a Bureau of Corporations to investigate companies suspected of antitrust violations and an Expedition Act to provide more funds to the attorney general to prosecute trusts. In 1903, Congress also passed the Elkins Act, named after Senator Stephen B. Elkins, outlawing railroad rebates to large companies.

Meanwhile, Roosevelt had decided to break up one of the largest trusts in the United States as a way of signaling his commitment to enforce the Sherman Antitrust Act. He directed his attorney general, Philander Knox, to prosecute the Northern Securities Company. This company had been formed by James Hill, head of the Great Northern Railroad; Edward Harriman, head of the Union Pacific Railroad; and the financier John Pierpont (J. P.) Morgan. The Northern Securities Company was a stockholding company that bought the stock of the two railroads. Through Northern Securities, Hill, Harriman, and Morgan controlled a large number of the rail lines from California to Chicago.

When Morgan heard that the government was going to try to break up the Northern Securities Company, he went to visit President Roosevelt and Attorney General Knox. Morgan believed that he could sit down with the president and that they could come up with a compromise like two businessmen. At first, Morgan suggested that they just make some slight changes in the structure of the company. According to Roosevelt's biographer Edmund Morris, the conversation went like this:

Roosevelt: That is just what we did not want to do.
Morgan: If we have done anything wrong, send your man to my man and they can fix it up.
Roosevelt: That can't be done.
Knox: We don't want to fix it up, we want to stop it.

In 1903, the case against Northern Securities reached the Supreme Court. Knox represented the federal government and argued that Northern Securities was not a stock company but a trust designed to restrict interstate commerce,

In 1903, President Teddy Roosevelt decided to take aim at the Northern Securities Company. J. P. Morgan (*white hair*), who was one of the founders, went to visit the president (*left*), hoping to settle the problem man to man. It didn't work out as he'd hoped. Secretary of War Elihu Root is seated between Roosevelt and Morgan. The fourth man is unidentified.

which was illegal under the Sherman Antitrust Act. In 1904, a majority of the Court agreed with the government's position. The majority decision in *Northern Securities Co. v. United States* was delivered by Associate Justice John Marshall Harlan, who stated that "the constituent companies ceased, under this arrangement, to be in active competition for trade and commerce along their respective lines, and became, practically, one powerful consolidated corporation . . . the arrangement was an illegal combination in restraint of interstate commerce. . . ." As a result of the Supreme Court's decision, the company was disbanded soon afterward.

After breaking up Northern Securities, Roosevelt decided to break up the Beef Trust, controlled by Gustavus Swift. The Bureau of Corporations had been investigating the Beef Trust and gathering the evidence necessary to bring a strong case against it. The case against the trust finally reached the Supreme Court in 1905. In the case of *Swift and Co. v. United States*, Associate Justice Oliver Wendell Holmes delivered the opinion of the Supreme Court. In this case, Holmes said that the company's business involved interstate commerce. Cattle were purchased in one state, shipped to another state for slaughter, and the beef was then transported by railcar to a third state for sale. It made no difference that parts of the operation—like the slaughterhouses—operated in only one state. This had been the position of the Supreme Court in *E. C. Knight*. Although sugar was sold in many states, it was refined in only one state, and, therefore, a monopoly of the refining plants was not considered part of interstate commerce. In addition, Holmes pointed out that the members of the trust conducted bidding to keep prices down and arranged to receive rebates from the railroads "to the exclusion of their competitors, with the intent to monopolize the commerce [in beef] among the States."

Therefore, according to Justice Holmes, Swift and Company's activities involved an effort to undermine the competition and create a monopoly—violations of the Sherman Act. Therefore, the Beef Trust must be broken up.

CHAPTER THREE

Standard Oil and Other Early Antitrust Cases

In November 1908, William Howard Taft was elected the twenty-seventh president of the United States. His presidency would redefine the Sherman Antitrust Act.

Born in Cincinnati, Ohio, in 1857, Taft attended what was then Yale College in New Haven, Connecticut, and graduated from the Cincinnati Law School. He later served as a judge on the U.S. Court of Appeals for the Sixth Circuit, where he handed down an important opinion in the *Addyston Pipe and Steel* antitrust case in 1898. That same year, the United States went to war with Spain and ceded the Spanish colony of the Philippines in the Pacific Ocean. President William McKinley selected Taft to head a commission to organize a new government for the Philippines, and he later became governor-general of the islands. After Taft's success governing the Philippines, President Roosevelt named Taft to be secretary of war in 1904, although he really wanted an appointment to the U.S. Supreme Court. Instead, Roosevelt chose Taft in

President William Howard Taft took up where President Theodore Roosevelt had left off in pursuing the large trusts in a case against Standard Oil that was decided by the Supreme Court—for the government and against the monopoly.

1908 to be the Republican nominee for president. Taft hated campaigning—"one of the most uncomfortable four months of my life," he said. Nevertheless, Taft won the election and took office the following year.

In 1909, the presidential inauguration was in March, not

in January as it is today. During his inaugural address, Taft pledged to carry on Roosevelt's work of breaking up the trusts. President Taft explained that Roosevelt's reforms "were directed to the suppression of the lawlessness and abuses of power of the great combinations of capital." Then he added: "To render the reforms lasting, however, and to secure at the same time freedom from alarm on the part of those pursuing proper and progressive business methods, further legislative and executive action are needed."

Under President Taft, the federal government continued to prosecute a case that had begun under President Roosevelt in 1906—the one involving Standard Oil. Before the Roosevelt administration had started working on the case, the state of Ohio had won a lawsuit against the company in the 1890s that required the breakup of a trust known as Standard Oil Company of Ohio. Standard Oil of Ohio, however, never actually gave up its control over many smaller companies. Eventually the trust simply changed its headquarters and re-formed itself under a new name, Standard Oil of New Jersey. This trust was just as formidable as the last one had been.

Standard Oil of New Jersey was considered a monopoly because of its enormous control over oil refining and selling it in the United States. The U.S. government took Standard Oil to court on charges of violating the Sherman Antitrust Act and won a decision against the company in U.S. Circuit Court in 1909. But Standard Oil of New Jersey appealed to the Supreme Court, which decided the case in 1911.

The 9 to 0 majority decision in the case, *Standard Oil of New Jersey Co. v. United States,* was delivered by Chief Justice Edward Douglass White. Reviewing the case, White said that the lawyers defending Standard Oil had argued that its success was due to "lawful competitive methods, guided by economic genius of the highest order, sustained by courage, by a keen insight into commercial situations, resulting in the acquisition of great wealth, but at the same time serving to stimulate and increase production, to widely extend the distribution of the products of petroleum at a cost largely below that which would have otherwise prevailed, thus proving to be . . . a benefaction to the general public. . . ."

In other words, according to the defense, Standard Oil had done nothing to restrain trade or achieve a monopoly that was illegal under the Sherman Act. Its success was due only to superior business methods, practices that the Sherman Act did not outlaw, and the company provided oil to consumers at very low prices.

The lower court, however, had disagreed with this defense, and the Supreme Court agreed with the decision of the lower court. Chief Justice White pointed out that after reviewing hundreds and hundreds of pages of evidence, he had concluded that the trust's "intent and purpose [was] to maintain the dominancy over the oil industry, not as a result of normal methods of industrial development, but by new means of combination which were resorted to in order that greater power might be added than would otherwise have arisen had normal methods been followed."

This included selling oil at extremely low prices to undercut competitors and drive them out of business and threatening any oil distributor who did business with a company other than Standard Oil. In a series of articles written for *McClure's* magazine from 1902 to 1904, writer Ida Tarbell had exposed many of the practices of Standard Oil. Tarbell was known as one of the muckrakers, writers and editors who revealed the corrupt practices of large American corporations. Tarbell exposed what she called the company's "open disregard

In the late nineteenth and early twentieth century, a group of investigative reporters known as "muckrakers" exposed the inhumane practices of the large corporations. Ida Tarbell, writing for *McClure*'s magazine, was influential in changing the way ordinary people viewed big business.

of decent ethical business practices by capitalists." And she added: "They had never played fair, and that ruined their greatness for me."

As a result of its decision, the Supreme Court ordered Standard Oil of New Jersey to be dissolved and broken up into the smaller companies that had comprised the trust. This would destroy the monopoly. The Court also ordered that the companies refrain from any of the trade-restraining acts that had been practiced by Standard Oil of New Jersey.

Nevertheless, while Standard Oil was dissolved, the Supreme Court pointed out that its decision did not mean that all business combinations were unlawful. As Justice White explained, any time one company buys another one and removes a competitor from the marketplace, competition is reduced. But this does not mean that a company in buying a competitor has violated the Sherman Antitrust Act, because many other competitors may still remain in a particular business area. Instead, White said that an interpretation of the Sherman Act required judges to use an "exercise of judgment," in deciding whether or not a combination of companies created a restraint of trade to create a monopoly. He called for judges to use "the standard of reason." This "rule of reason," as it has been called, required that judges look at each case to decide whether it involved a violation of the rules governing restraint of trade in order to create a monopoly. Not every combination of companies was a violation of those rules.

DR. MILES MEDICAL COMPANY

In the same year as the *Standard Oil* decision, the Supreme Court decided another important antitrust case: *Dr. Miles Medical Co. v. John D. Park & Sons Co.* Dr. Miles Medical Company was located in Indiana and sold its medicines in the United States and abroad to wholesale drug companies as well as to retail drugstores. Dr. Miles signed agreements with wholesalers requiring them to sell the drugs at the same price or higher than the price charged by Dr. Miles to the wholesale companies. In addition, the retail drugstores had to sell Dr. Miles's products at the prices that were printed on the drug packages. Thus Dr. Miles had set the minimum price at which the company's products could be sold.

John D. Park & Sons was a Kentucky company in the whole-sale drug business. Park had obtained products from Dr. Miles but refused to sign any agreement with the company. Instead, according to Dr. Miles, Park was selling the drugs at less than the prices specified by the Dr. Miles Company. In addition, Dr. Miles charged that Park obtained its products from other retailers and wholesalers that had signed agreements with Dr. Miles. Then they had been persuaded by Park to disregard the agreements. These medicines were advertised and sold by Park for less than the prices on Dr. Miles's drug packages.

In a Supreme Court decision delivered by Associate Justice Charles Evans Hughes, a majority decided that Dr. Miles had tried "to control not merely the prices at which its agents may sell its products, but the prices for all sales by all dealers at wholesale or retail . . . and thus to fix the amount which the consumer shall pay, eliminating all competition. . . . Thus all room for competition between retailers, who supply the public, is made impossible. . . . That these agreements restrain trade is obvious." And the Court therefore ordered that Dr. Miles must eliminate them.

Minimum resale prices were considered by the Supreme Court as a *per se* violation of the Sherman Antitrust Act. That is, by themselves, any attempt by a company to enforce minimum pricing among retailers eliminated retail competition. Minimum pricing did not have to be considered under the rule of reason. It was always illegal, regardless of the circumstances. This was also an example of vertical price fixing—that is, an attempt to control prices at various levels of sale—wholesaling as well as retail. The Sherman Act outlawed vertical price fixing.

The Clayton Antitrust Act and

In 1912, Democrat Woodrow Wilson was elected president, and he wanted to extend the power of the Sherman Antitrust Act. The Sherman Act had generally prohibited monopolies and restraints on competition. The Clayton Antitrust Act, named after Congressman Henry Clayton of Alabama and passed in 1914, was more specific. The Clayton Antitrust Act prohibited price discrimination. That is, the act prevented a seller involved in interstate commerce from offering the same type and quality of product to two different buyers at two different prices if price discrimination was designed to reduce or eliminate competition. In addition, the Clayton Antitrust Act outlawed exclusive dealing. This prohibited a company from insisting that a buyer must deal with it exclusively and could not purchase similar products from other companies. Under the Clayton Antitrust Act, this was an effort to reduce competition and create a monopoly.

The Clayton Antitrust Act also prohibited tying arrangements. These required a buyer who wanted one product to purchase another, less desirable product that might have been purchased at a lower price somewhere else. For example, a buyer who wanted to purchase a supply of quality soft drinks from a beverage company would be forced to purchase a supply of another soft drink that was inferior to it. The Clayton Antitrust Act also stated that a purchaser who won a case against a seller should receive triple damages— that is, three times the amount of money that was lost by the purchaser because the seller had violated the law.

In 1914, Congress also passed the Federal Trade Commission Act. The new law established a commission to enforce the Clayton Antitrust Act. It consisted of five commissioners appointed by the president. The Federal Trade Commission (FTC) was also given authority to investigate possible

the Federal Trade Commission Act

In 1914, the Clayton Antitrust Act was passed. Named after Alabama Congressman Henry Clayton, shown here walking (*left*). it prohibited price discrimination.

violations of antitrust law, hold hearings on them with the organizations involved, and, if necessary, issue orders—called cease and desist orders—telling the organizations to stop those actions that led to the violations.

FEDERAL BASEBALL CLUB OF BALTIMORE AND TRENTON POTTERIES

Antitrust cases continued to reach the Supreme Court during the 1920s. One of the most interesting cases involved Major League Baseball—*Federal Baseball Club of Baltimore, Inc.* v. *National League of Professional Baseball Clubs.* Founded in 1913, the Federal Baseball League consisted of eight professional teams. Four of these teams were located in cities that already had baseball clubs in the National or American Leagues, which had been organized earlier. Following the 1915 season, the Federal League was struggling, and several of the teams were purchased by the National League owners. What was left of the league could not survive. One of the teams still in the league that had not been purchased was the Baltimore Terrapins. Its owner sued the other two leagues for trying to buy as many teams as possible and create a baseball monopoly, putting the Federal League out of business. This was a violation of the Sherman Antitrust Act, according to the owner of the Terrapins.

In a lower court, the Terrapins' owner won the case and received triple damages under the Clayton Antitrust Act, amounting to $240,000, a huge sum at the time. The case was appealed by the National League owners, eventually reaching the Supreme Court. In a unanimous decision handed down by Associate Justice Oliver Wendell Holmes in 1922, the Court decided that the National League owners had not violated the Sherman Antitrust Act.

Justice Holmes ruled that baseball did not involve interstate commerce. Although teams did have to travel from one state to another, he said that the actual games were played within a single state. Their "business is giving exhibitions of baseball, which are purely state affairs." The Court's decision

The Brooklyn Federal League baseball club, shown here in 1914, was part of the league that became involved in a suit that went as far as the Supreme Court. However, the Court ruled that baseball clubs did not fall under antitrust laws because they were not considered to involve interstate commerce.

effectively enabled the National and American Leagues to have a monopoly of big league baseball that would continue to affect the sport and its players during the decades ahead.

Five years later, in 1927, Associate Justice Harlan Fiske Stone handed down another majority decision in the important case of *United States* v. *Trenton Potteries Company*. This case involved twenty-three companies that were members of the Sanitary Potters' Association, makers of toilet bowls and other products. They had been charged with forming a trade group to fix—control—prices across their industry. That is horizontal price fixing—a *per se* violation of the Sherman Antitrust Act. In this case, Stone pointed out that the rule of reason did not apply to controlling prices. The Potters' Association had argued that the prices they charged their buyers were reasonable. But Stone said that this was not a legitimate reason to permit price fixing. As Justice Stone put it, "it does not follow that agreements to fix or maintain prices are reasonable restraints and therefore permitted... merely because the prices themselves are reasonable.... The aim and result of every price-fixing agreement, if effective, is the elimination of one form of competition. . . . The reasonable price fixed today may through economic and business changes become the unreasonable price of tomorrow. Once established, it may be maintained unchanged because of the absence of competition. . . ."

Stone and a majority of the court ruled that any conspiracy by a company or group of companies to get together and control prices was a violation of the Sherman Antitrust Act. Controlling prices—that is, price fixing—was an effort to eliminate competition in pricing and force the consumer to pay a single price. With decisions in important cases such as *Standard Oil of New Jersey, Dr. Miles Medical Company, Federal Baseball Club*, and *Trenton Potteries,* the Supreme Court had interpreted and defined the meaning of the Sherman Antitrust Act in terms of monopolies and price fixing. The decisions in these cases provided fair warning to any organization that might consider engaging in the practices that were outlawed under the Sherman or the Clayton Antitrust Acts.

CHAPTER FOUR

The Great Depression and the Labor Unions

In October 1929, the New York Stock Exchange suffered an enormous collapse, and the United States began to sink into the Great Depression. Banks closed, depositors lost their life savings, businesses went bankrupt, and eventually 25 percent of American workers were thrown out of their jobs. The Republican administration of President Herbert Hoover seemed unable to deal with the massive unemployment caused by the Depression, and in 1932 Americans overwhelmingly elected Democrat Franklin Roosevelt president. Beginning in 1933, a number of important cases involving the Sherman Act were decided by the courts, several of which concerned labor unions.

In March 1933, shortly after Roosevelt was inaugurated, the Supreme Court decided an important antitrust case that reflected the economic conditions of the Great Depression. The case involved 137 coal producers in Virginia, West Virginia, Kentucky, and Tennessee. They had formed an

The election of Franklin Delano Roosevelt as the United States sank into a Great Depression led to the beginning of a great era for the working class, and restrictions on the very wealthy.

organization called Appalachian Coals to sell their coal to customers at the best possible prices in a depressed market. The coal was used as a fuel to heat homes and businesses. Sales in the coal industry had been declining as a result of the Depression and competition from other sources of fuel such as oil and natural gas. Far more coal was being produced than could be purchased by American consumers.

After hearing the case, the U.S. District Court in Virginia ruled that Appalachian Coals was in violation of the Sherman Antitrust Act. Since the coal producers controlled about 75 percent of the coal in their area and they had combined to determine prices, their organization appeared to be creating a restraint of trade and driving out competition. The district court stated that Appalachian Coals would "have a tendency to stabilize prices and to raise prices to a higher level than would prevail under conditions of free competition." Therefore, the court ordered that Appalachian Coals should cease operation.

However, the Supreme Court saw the case differently. In the majority opinion for *Appalachian Coals, Inc. v. United States*, Chief Justice Charles Evans Hughes described the terrible economic conditions that existed in the coal industry. He added that many companies had gone into bankruptcy, shutting down mines, cutting wages for some miners, and forcing many others out of jobs. Representatives of railroads in the area, which carried coal to customers, as well as other coal producers, had testified in District Court that Appalachian Coals would not stifle competition. Hughes also pointed out that "only a small percentage" of their product was actually sold in the area where the mines were located. Most of it was sold in other parts of the United States where there was tremendous competition from other coal companies.

Finally, Hughes emphasized that the Sherman Act must be interpreted by "the essential standard of reasonableness. . . . A cooperative enterprise is not to be condemned as an undue restraint because it may effect a change in market conditions, where the change would be in mitigation of recognized evils and would not impair, but rather would foster, fair competitive opportunities." The justices reversed the ruling of the

As Chief Justice of the Supreme Court, Charles Evans Hughes decided in favor of the coal industry in *Appalachian Coals, Inc.* v. *United States.* It was this type of decision by conservative judges that would lead President Roosevelt to try to "pack" the Court with younger, more liberal justices later in his presidency. The attempt failed, but the tenor of the Court changed with the times.

District Court, believing that Appalachian Coals promoted the strength of the coal industry, preserved jobs at a time of severe economic depression, and did not drive out competition. Thus, in making its decision, the court did not say that price fixing was a *per se* violation of the Sherman Act. The majority of the Supreme Court took existing economic conditions into account. This was an important change in the Court's interpretation of the Sherman Act.

While the profits of the coal mining industry took a hit during the Depression, the coal miners themselves endured long hours in dangerous mines, and were exposed to toxins that often led to significant lung disease or premature death.

THE RISE OF THE LABOR UNIONS

A few days before the *Appalachian Coals* decision, President Franklin Roosevelt delivered his inaugural address. In an effort to instill confidence during the depths of the Great Depression, Roosevelt told the American people that the "only thing we have to fear is fear itself." His administration proposed a series of programs designed to reduce fear of America's economic future and put people back to work. Called the New Deal, it included a number of initiatives—building roads and bridges, and refurbishing city parks and playgrounds—that would provide work for hundreds

Loewe v. Lawlor

In support of this position, the Supreme Court had delivered a unanimous opinion in the case of *Loewe* v. *Lawlor* in 1908. Chief Justice Melville Weston Fuller wrote the opinion for the Court. He stated that the United Hatters Union of North America and their business agent Martin Lawlor had violated the Sherman Antitrust Act. The United Hatters had encouraged members of other unions across the United States to boycott, or not to purchase, hats made by the Danbury (Connecticut) Hatters, owned by D. E. Loewe and Company. The union took this action because Loewe would not permit the United Hatters to form a union at the company.

The United Hatters were a national union with approximately 9,000 members engaged in manufacturing hats. About one third of the union's hatters worked in Connecticut, a center of the hat-manufacturing business. A small union, the Hatters had joined the much larger American Federation of Labor (AFL)—a union with more than one million members in 1908. With the help of the AFL, the Hatters called for a boycott of Loewe's hats, which did not carry the union label. The union also stated in its case before the Supreme Court that Loewe had fired any of their employees who had joined the United Hatters and hired nonunion workers to replace them.

Loewe and Company responded that the United Hatters along with the AFL were unlawfully restraining its business under the Sherman Antitrust Act. Loewe's lawyers argued that this was no different than a large trust trying to force a smaller competitor out of the marketplace. The Supreme

Court agreed and ordered the United Hatters to pay Loewe $252,000, three times the amount of money lost to the company as a result of the boycott. This sent a message to other unions that the Supreme Court would try to reduce their power to deal with large employers.

To deal with this problem, unions tried to influence Congress to pass new legislation that might help them. The result was passage of the Clayton Antitrust Act in 1914. Section 6 of the act states: "The labor of human beings is not a commodity or article of commerce. Nothing contained in the antitrust laws shall be construed to forbid the existence and operation of labor . . . organizations . . . nor shall such organizations, or members thereof, be held or construed to be illegal combinations or conspiracies in restraint of trade, under the antitrust laws."

of thousands of Americans. The administration also established an Antitrust Division of the Department of Justice to prosecute cases under the Sherman Act and the Clayton Act.

At the same time, Congress had begun passing new legislation aimed at protecting labor unions. Large labor unions had arisen during the late nineteenth century, organizing millions of workers so they could deal with the powerful corporations that employed them. Business owners routinely required their employees to work twelve-hour days, employing child labor on dangerous machinery in their factories. Corporations provided no retirement programs, health benefits, or workmen's compensation for employees who had been injured on the job and could not work. Unions tried to change these conditions, going on strike and shutting down manufacturing plants in an effort to force employers to improve wages and working conditions.

Employers tried to break the strikes by bringing in armed guards to battle the unions. The guards tried to prevent union members from picketing work sites, bringing their operations to a standstill and preventing nonunion employees from going to work in the manufacturing plants. In addition, employers resorted to the power of law courts to stop the unions. "Yellow-dog" contracts, which prohibited workers from being employed if they were union members, were legal according to the courts. Another tool that employers used was the Sherman Antitrust Act. They claimed that unions, by going on strike at large corporations that were engaged in interstate commerce, were restraining trade by shutting down plants so they could no longer manufacture and sell their products.

In 1932, during the depths of the Great Depression, Congress passed the Norris–La Guardia Act. Named after Sena-

Senator George Norris of Nebraska and Congressman Fiorello La Guardia of New York pushed for a bill that outlawed "yellow-dog contracts," which prohibited workers from organizing unions and from going on strike.

tor George Norris of Nebraska and Congressman Fiorello La Guardia of New York, the law stated that yellow-dog contracts were no longer legal. It prohibited federal courts from issuing orders requested by employers that prevented workers from organizing a union and going on strike. Following this law, Congress passed the National Labor Relations Act in 1935, which reinforced many of the provisions of the Norris–La Guardia Act. It also established the National Labor Relations Board, with members appointed by the president. The board monitored union elections and determined whether a union had fairly won an election among employees at a particular company. If so, the company could not prevent the union from representing the employees who worked there.

In the past, many companies had tried to prevent unions from holding elections and representing employees. As a result of these laws, union membership grew from about 3.5 million in 1935 to 10.2 million by the early 1940s.

In 1940, the Supreme Court considered *Apex Hosiery Co. v. Leader,* a case that involved the application of the Sherman Antitrust Act to union activities. A union had called a strike at a Pennsylvania stocking factory, Apex Hosiery, in 1937. The strike prevented more than 1.5 million finished stockings valued at about $800,000 from being shipped to customers in other states. A lower court had ruled that the strike was a violation of the Sherman Act and awarded the company more than $700,000 in damages. The Supreme Court reversed this decision in an opinion that was delivered by Associate Justice Harlan Fiske Stone.

Stone wrote:

> Here it is plain that the combination [the labor union] did not have as its purpose restraint upon competition in the market for . . . the product. Its object was to compel petitioner [Apex] to accede to the union demands. . . . So far as appears the delay of these shipments was not intended to have and had no effect on prices of hosiery in the market, and so was in that respect no more a restraint forbidden by the Sherman Act than the restriction upon competition and the course of trade held lawful in *Appalachian Coals, Inc. v. United States.* . . .

The Supreme Court had upheld the right of unions to strike for better wages and working conditions for its members. While the Danbury Hatters decision had reduced the power of the unions, *Apex Hosiery* increased their power.

The Supreme Court reached a similar conclusion in *United States* v. *Hutcheson* in 1941. William Hutcheson was head of the United Brotherhood of Carpenters and Joiners of America. The federal government claimed in this case that union activities, including strikes and resistance to new labor-saving technology on construction jobs, were violations of the Sherman Antitrust Act. In the majority opinion delivered by Associate Justice Felix Frankfurter, the Supreme Court stated that the union's actions were protected by the Norris–La Guardia Act and the Clayton Antitrust Act. These permitted the right of unions to strike for higher wages and improved working conditions.

EXEMPTIONS UNDER THE SHERMAN ACT

The author and antitrust lawyer Richard Pogue wrote that unions received an exemption under the Sherman Antitrust Act after the passage of the Clayton Act and the Norris–La Guardia Act, as well as the Supreme Court decisions in *Apex* and *Hutcheson.*

In addition to labor unions, the agencies of the federal and state governments also are exempt from the Sherman Act if they are involved in controlling prices—something that would be considered illegal if done by a private corporation. This position was upheld in 1943, when Justice Stone delivered the majority opinion in the case of *Parker, Director of Agriculture, et al.* v. *Brown.* The case involved Brown, a raisin producer in California, who brought a case against the state when it set up a program to establish a national marketing program for raisins and set prices to be charged by California growers. The intent of the program was to improve sales and prevent destructive competition among growers. Justice Stone wrote that this was not a violation of the Sherman Act because it involved an action by a state. This became known as the *Parker* v. *Brown* rule.

TYING AND MONOPOLIES

The practice of tying—selling one product and requiring a customer to purchase another one—is prohibited under the Sherman Antitrust Act and the Clayton Antitrust Act. In 1936, the Supreme Court clearly stated its position against tying in the case of *International Business Machines Corp.* v. *United States*. International Business Machines (IBM) had patented some of the earliest computers. A patent gives a company or individual exclusive ownership of an invention for a specific period of time, usually twenty years. Under the patent, no one else can sell or lease [rent] the machinery to customers. IBM required any company that bought the computer to use specially designed cards so the computer would operate properly. The punched cards were used to input information. These cards were not patented by IBM and could just as easily be purchased from other suppliers. According to the Clayton Antitrust Act, no company could require a customer that leased machinery to use supplies that could be provided by a competitor. This was tying and considered a restraint of competition, and IBM was ordered to stop requiring customers to purchase its cards.

The Supreme Court reaffirmed its position in the case of *International Salt Co.* v. *United States* in 1947. In the *International Salt* case, the company had patented industrial machines. These were used to create saltwater and to inject salt into canned food to preserve it. International Salt also required companies using its machines to purchase its salt. However, the same quality salt could just as easily have been purchased from other salt companies. Associate Justice

People disagreed on politics, but almost everyone in twentieth century America loved the movies. In 1948, however, the Supreme Court ruled against price fixing by the major motion picture studios.

Robert Jackson delivered the majority opinion stating that the company's action was a violation of laws prohibiting tying because it was aimed at eliminating competition. This was considered a *per se* violation of the Sherman Act and the Clayton Act.

A year later, in 1948, the Supreme Court delivered a landmark decision that affected motion pictures. *United States v. Paramount Pictures, Inc.* was a case that involved vertical integration, monopoly, and price fixing—all violations of the

The Antitrust Division, FTC,

Soon after coming to office in 1933, the Roosevelt Administration created the Antitrust Division of the U.S. Department of Justice. This division was given the authority to initiate investigations into possible antitrust violations of the Sherman Act and the Clayton Act. To carry out these investigations, the Antitrust Division begins with a preliminary inquiry, looking for information about an organization suspected of violations, speaking to any competitor or individual who believes the organization has violated antitrust law, and finally deciding whether to proceed with a formal civil or criminal investigation. In civil cases, if an organization is found to have violated antitrust law, it is sued in court, and if the government wins the suit, the organization must stop its activities and often pay a fine. In criminal cases, the Antitrust Division brings its evidence before a grand jury. A grand jury is a jury that listens to the evidence and decides whether it is strong enough to charge someone with a crime. In criminal cases, top executives involved in antitrust violations may also be sent to prison if they are found guilty.

An antitrust investigation can also be initiated by the Federal Trade Commission. In 2007, for example, the Whole Foods grocery chain and a smaller competitor, Wild Oats, announced a merger. The FTC successfully challenged the merger, saying that the new company would control too large a part of the natural foods market, stifling competition.

Finally, under the antitrust laws, individuals can bring lawsuits against firms. Frequently, these are class action

and Private Lawsuits

In 2007, the Federal Trade Commission denied the bid of the Whole Foods chain to take over Wild Oats, a smaller "health-foods" grocery chain, saying that the merger would stifle competition.

lawsuits. That is, they are brought against an organization by a lawyer representing a group of people who may have been harmed by a violation of the antitrust law, such as price fixing.

Sherman Act. The case involved America's largest movie studios—not only Paramount, but also Twentieth Century Fox, Columbia Pictures, Universal Pictures, and Warner Bros.

In the 1940s, the major motion picture studios owned many of the theaters where films were shown. Other theaters were partnerships between the film studios and local owners. All of these theaters were doing almost one half of the movie business in the United States. To enhance their business, the studios were involved in practices that the federal government believed were violations of the Sherman Act. Some of the theaters were owned by two movie studios that were in competition with each other. The movie studios also required local theater owners to take a whole group of movies, without screening them in advance, instead of being able to select only the movies they wanted. In addition, the movie studios worked together to fix admission prices at various theaters. Finally, the studios refused to rent movies to small independent theaters that were not owned by the large studios.

In the majority decision, written by Associate Justice William O. Douglas, the Supreme Court said that these activities by the movie studios resulted in "stifling competition and diverting the cream of the business to the large operators." As a result of this decision, known as the *Paramount* Decrees, the production of films and the ownership of theater businesses were required to become independent of each other.

CHAPTER FIVE

Monopolies and Price Fixing, 1950s–1960s

During the 1950s and 1960s, there were a number of important antitrust cases involving monopolies, covered under Section I of the Sherman Antitrust Act, and price fixing, covered under Section II of the act. One of these cases related to Major League Baseball and a pitcher named George Earl Toolson.

Toolson was a minor league pitcher who played for the Newark Bears. The Bears were a farm team for the New York Yankees. Toolson wanted to play for the Yankees, but they did not call him up to their team. Because he was under contract to the Yankees, Toolson was not permitted to look for a job with another big league team. Even after his contract expired, Toolson was forced to abide by the baseball reserve clause. The reserve clause stated that for another year after his contract expired, Toolson had to play for the Yankees or they could trade him to another team. In short, they controlled his career.

Whitey Ford was a famous New York Yankees player in the 1950s and 1960s. Because Major League Baseball was exempt from the Sherman Antitrust Act, baseball players were basically owned by their teams for most of the twentieth century.

The Yankees decided to keep Toolson and sent him to the Binghamton Triplets—a Double A Yankee farm team, a lower class than the Triple A Bears. But Toolson refused to go and decided to challenge the reserve clause. Toolson claimed that by preventing him and all other players from making a deal with another team, the Major League Baseball clubs were exercising a monopoly over their players' careers. This was a violation of the Sherman Act. A player's right to engage in interstate commerce and join a team in another state was being restricted by the reserve clause.

Decades earlier, the baseball major leagues had received an exemption from the provisions of the Sherman Act in the

Federal Baseball Club of Baltimore v. *National League of Professional Baseball Clubs* decision. When the *Toolson* case was tried in the lower courts, the judges cited the *Federal Baseball Club* decision and ruled against Toolson, saying that he had to abide by the reserve clause. Toolson appealed the decision, and the case eventually reached the Supreme Court.

In a 7 to 2 decision, delivered in 1953, the Court upheld the lower courts' decision in *Toolson* v. *New York Yankees*. According to the majority of the justices, "the business of providing public baseball games for profit between clubs of professional baseball players was not within the scope of the federal antitrust laws. Congress has had the ruling under consideration, but has not seen fit to bring such business under these laws by legislation. . . . The business has thus been left for thirty years to develop on the understanding that it was not subject to existing antitrust legislation."

The Supreme Court and the lower courts are usually reluctant to overturn a previous decision. Instead the courts are guided by these earlier precedents. This is called the rule of *stare decisis.* While recognizing that conditions in Major League Baseball had changed since the earlier case, the Court left it to Congress to pass new legislation affecting Major League Baseball, ending its exemption under the Sherman Antitrust Act. The justices believed that this was the responsibility of Congress under the Constitution, not the role of the Supreme Court.

Associate Justice Harold Burton was one of two justices who dissented from the decision. In a strongly worded minority opinion, he said, "Whatever may have been the situation when the *Federal Baseball Club* case was decided in 1922, I am not able to join today's decision, which, in effect, announces that organized baseball, in 1953, still is not engaged in interstate trade or commerce. In the light of organized baseball's well known and widely distributed capital investments used in conducting competitions between teams constantly traveling between states . . . its radio and television activities which expand its audiences beyond state lines, its sponsorship of interstate advertising, and its highly organized 'farm system' of minor league baseball clubs . . . it is a contradiction in terms to say that the defendants in the cases before us are not now engaged in interstate trade or commerce as those terms are used in the Constitution of the United States and in the Sherman Act."

While the Supreme Court had given baseball an exemption under the Sherman Act, the justices did not apply the same exemption to other professional sports. In 1938, William Radovich became a guard for the Detroit Lions, a professional team in the National Football League (NFL). After playing several seasons with the Lions, Radovich wanted to be traded to the Los Angeles Rams, where he could receive more money and play near the home of his parents. Radovich's contract with the Lions had expired, but they refused to trade him to the Rams. So he left the National Football League to play for a rival league, the All-American Football Conference. As a result, Detroit owner Fred Madel Jr. put Radovich on a blacklist. This prevented him from playing with any team associated with the National Football League. The intent of the blacklist was also to make it difficult for players to leave the league and jump to a rival. This prevented another league from acquiring good players and challenging the NFL.

In 1948, the San Francisco Clippers of the Pacific Coast League, which was associated with the NFL, wanted to hire Radovich as a player/coach. But when the team found out

Challenging the Reserve Clause

The Major League Baseball teams had begun using the reserve clause in the late nineteenth century. It was designed to prevent players from negotiating with a variety of teams in an effort to receive the highest possible salaries. Team owners were afraid that high salaries might bankrupt their operations. On the other hand, the players argued that the reserve clause gave teams too much control over their careers. Even when their contracts ended, they were not free to negotiate. This gave their teams an opportunity to re-sign them at any price that was being offered. At the end of the next contract, a team could invoke the reserve clause once again, controlling a player indefinitely.

In 1969, St. Louis Cardinal star outfielder Curt Flood challenged the reserve clause when he refused to report to the Philadelphia Phillies after being traded to their team. In the case of *Flood* v. *Kuhn* (Bowie Kuhn was the commissioner of baseball), the Supreme Court handed down a 5 to 3 decision in 1972 that upheld the validity of the reserve clause.

Later in the 1970s, major league pitchers Andy Messersmith and Dave McNally refused to sign their contracts and played for a year without them. They claimed that the reserve clause was no longer valid after a year, and they could become free agents negotiating a new contract with any team. An arbitrator assigned by Major League Baseball to decide the case agreed with the two players. Eventually the reserve clause was changed, allowing players who had been with the same team for six years to become free agents. This meant that they could negotiate with any team for a new contract.

that he had been blacklisted, they withdrew their offer. Radovich, without any job in professional football, decided to challenge the blacklisting. He pointed out that he had been the victim of practices by the NFL designed to monopolize professional football. In response, the NFL said that it was doing nothing different than professional baseball.

In 1957, *Radovich* v. *National Football League* reached the Supreme Court. The decision, written by Associate Justice Tom Clark, said that the "rule established in *Federal Baseball Club* v. *National League* and *Toolson* v. *New York Yankees* is specifically limited to the business of organized professional baseball and does not control this case. As long as Congress continues to acquiesce, this Court should adhere to—but not extend—the interpretation of the [Sherman] Act made in those cases. . . . The volume of interstate business involved in organized professional football places it within the provisions of the Antitrust Acts."

The *Radovich* case meant that professional football was to be treated differently from major league baseball under the Sherman Act. In fact, baseball has always been an exception that does not apply to other sports. Players like Radovich could leave when their contracts expired and play for other teams or play in rival leagues, giving these leagues the opportunity to build teams and compete against the NFL. Several leagues did compete, including the American Football League, which eventually merged with the NFL. Other competing leagues have included the World Football League and the United States Football League.

OTHER MONOPOLY CASES

In looking at a possible monopoly under the Sherman Act, the courts consider both the geographical areas in which organizations or companies are operating and the type of businesses that they are conducting.

For example, in 1955 the Supreme Court heard the case of *United States* v. *E. I. DuPont de Nemours & Co.* DuPont controlled 75 percent of the U.S. market for cellophane wrap, which is used to cover and preserve food. This appeared to give DuPont a monopoly of the market among American consumers. But in an opinion delivered by Associate Justice Stanley Reed, the Court ruled that the market was much broader than just cellophane. Reed pointed out that there were substitutes for cellophane, such as aluminum foil, that could be used instead of cellophane wrap. Since DuPont controlled only 20 percent of this market, it had not violated the monopoly provisions of the Sherman Act.

The Sherman Act is not only aimed at eliminating existing monopolies; it also tries to prevent companies from attempting to monopolize a particular industry. In 1957, the U. S. Court of Appeals heard the case of *Kansas City Star Company* v. *United States.* The case involved three newspapers owned by the Star Company in Kansas City, Missouri. The company also owned a local radio station and television station. The *Star* told any customer who wanted to advertise in its newspapers or on its radio or television station that it would not accept the advertising if the customer was also placing ads in the publications of the *Star*'s competitors. For example, the owner of three movie theaters was informed that if he advertised in a rival newspaper, the *Star* would not accept his ads. In addition, advertisers who wanted to run commercials on the Star Company's radio and television stations were told that they must also run ads in the newspapers.

When the case came before the lower court, it ruled that the Star Company had violated the Sherman Antitrust Act because it was attempting to monopolize advertising in the Kansas City market. The Star Company then appealed the decision. But the Court of Appeals agreed with the lower court, saying that the company had attempted by illegal means to monopolize advertising in the Kansas City media market. As the court put it, "The phrase 'attempt to monopolize' means the employment of methods, means and practices which would, if successful, accomplish monopolization, and which, though falling short, nevertheless approach so close as to create a dangerous probability of it." The Star Company was trying to monopolize the media market in Kansas City, a clear violation of the Sherman Act. Although the Star Company had not yet become a monopoly, the court ruled that it must stop any practices aimed at achieving a monopoly position.

VERTICAL AND HORIZONTAL PRICE FIXING

In addition to the cases regarding monopolies, the courts continued to enforce the Sherman Act in cases involving Section I of the act—restraints of trade by controlling prices. In one case, *United States* v. *Parke, Davis and Co.* (1960), the Supreme Court cited a precedent that had been set more than forty years earlier. This was a case of vertical price fixing, *United States* v. *Colgate & Co.*, in 1919. Colgate, a manufacturer of pharmaceutical products, had been sending letters to its customers—wholesalers and retailers—announcing the prices that must be charged for the company's products. It also stopped dealing with those customers if they refused to follow the company pricing policies.

But in *Colgate* there had been no contracts to fix prices, which were specifically prohibited by the Sherman Act. Earlier, in 1911, the Supreme Court had found in the *Dr. Miles*

In 1960, the Sherman Antitrust Act was invoked in a case against the pharmaceutical company, Parke–Davis, which was found to be guilty of not only announcing minimum prices for its products but of forcing wholesalers and retailers to apply these prices— or else!

case that the Miles company had violated the Sherman Act by requiring its customers to sign written contracts agreeing to the company's pricing policies. But the Supreme Court said that Colgate had not violated the act by simply announcing prices—with no written contracts—and then refusing to deal with those customers who did not follow them. The Colgate Doctrine, as it became known, was a narrow interpretation of the Sherman Act, to be sure, but the Supreme Court often interprets cases very narrowly.

In the *Parke, Davis* case, however, the Supreme Court said

that the Colgate Doctrine did not apply. Parke–Davis not only announced the minimum prices for their products, but company representatives went to wholesalers to make sure that they charged the suggested prices. In addition, these representatives said that Parke–Davis would no longer deal with the wholesalers if they did not stick to these prices or if they sold to retail pharmacies that did not follow the pricing policies. Parke–Davis then stopped dealing with any retailers that did not charge the minimum prices.

In a 6 to 3 decision delivered by Associate Justice William Brennan, the Supreme Court stated that the company "did not merely announce its policy and then decline to have further dealings with retailers who failed to abide by it, but, by utilizing wholesalers . . . it actively induced unwilling retailers to comply with the policy. The resulting concerted action to maintain the resale prices constituted a conspiracy or combination in violation of the Sherman Act." Section I of the Sherman Act specifically prohibits conspiracies and combinations by businesses to control prices.

While this case was being decided, General Motors Corporation had become involved in a similar situation that would eventually be decided by the Supreme Court. Starting in the 1950s, a dozen Chevrolet dealers in Los Angeles, California, had been selling automobiles to "discount houses" that were advertising the cars at reduced prices. These discount dealers began taking business away from the eighty-five Chevrolet dealers in the Los Angeles area. These dealers, who belonged to Losor Chevrolet Dealers Association, complained to two of the dealers who were selling to the discount houses, but they refused to stop. Losor then wrote letters to General Motors, which decided to talk to the dealers who were selling to the discount houses. One dealer, Wilber Newman, was visited by

Today we look at the Chevy Impala as a classic American car. In 1966, Chevrolets were at the center of a restraint-of-trade case decided against its owner, General Motors, by the Supreme Court.

Roy Cash, the regional manager for Chevrolet. Newman later explained that in a meeting with Cash, the regional manager said that he would treat those dealers selling to discount houses the same way that he treated children.

To ensure that the dealers complied with Cash's orders, Losor and General Motors hired a private detective to travel around to discounters, posing as a car buyer, to see if they were still selling discounted Chevrolets. General Motors then brought in any dealer still selling to discounters for a face-to-face meeting and pressured them to change their policies. In every case, the dealer bought back the cars that he had sold to the discount houses. By early 1961, no more Chevrolets were being sold to discounters.

FTC and Unfair Competition

Antitrust cases, such as *United States* v. *General Motors Corp.*, can begin in a variety of ways. In the General Motors case, a federal grand jury was assembled by the Department of Justice to look into the activities of General Motors and Losor. A case can also be brought by the Federal Trade Commission after it has received complaints by business owners who believe that their businesses have been hurt by competitors who are violating the Sherman Antitrust Act. Established in 1914, the FTC is an agency of the federal government tasked with ensuring that business competition in the United States remains fair. The FTC can look into the complaint and, if there is enough evidence, bring the case in front of an administrative law judge for a decision. Some of these decisions are appealed and may eventually reach the Supreme Court.

In one case, *Federal Trade Commission* v. *Brown Shoe Co., Inc.* (1966), the FTC had filed a complaint against Brown Shoe, America's second-largest shoe manufacturer. The complaint stated that the company had persuaded 650 of its customers—retail shoe stores—to sign an agreement to restrict them from buying shoes from other manufacturers. In return, they received special benefits such as the right to participate in a group health insurance program with lower rates than each store owner was currently paying. The FTC said that Brown Shoe was engaging in unfair competition by preventing competitors from selling to hundreds of retail stores and ordered it to stop this activity. Brown Shoe appealed the case and it eventually reached the Supreme Court. In a unanimous decision handed down by Associate Justice Hugo Black, the Court said that Brown's activities violated the Sherman Act as well as the Clayton Act, and the FTC had the power to stop them.

Nevertheless, the Supreme Court ruled in *United States* v. *General Motors Corp.* (1966) that the practice of buying back the discounted cars must stop. In a decision delivered by Associate Justice Abraham Fortas, the Court said that it was "a classic conspiracy in restraint of trade: joint, collaborative action by dealers . . . associations, and General Motors to eliminate a class of competitors by terminating dealings between them and a minority of Chevrolet dealers and to deprive franchised dealers of their freedom to deal through discounters if they so choose." Under the Sherman Act this is considered a refusal to deal with a competitor to eliminate him from the marketplace—a *per se* violation. As Fortas said, "Exclusion of traders from the market by means of a combination or conspiracy is . . . inconsistent with the free-market principles embodied in the Sherman Act. . . ." In his decision, Justice Fortas also cited the *Parke, Davis* case, saying that General Motors had tried to "elicit from all the dealers agreements . . . that none of them would do business with discounters. These agreements were hammered out in meetings. . . ." In other words, General Motors and the Losor Association had conspired in agreements to prevent discount dealers from doing business. They were ordered to stop the policy of prohibiting sales to discounters.

Ray Kroc launched McDonald's, but it's unlikely that he ever imagined that McDonald's would one day have almost one million individual stores all over the world.

CHAPTER SIX

Franchising and the Sherman Act

During the 1960s and 1970s, franchising became very popular. An entrepreneur, known as a franchisee, could purchase a franchise from a company known as the franchisor. Well-known franchisors included companies such as McDonald's, Baskin-Robbins, and Midas muffler shops. By 2010, there were an estimated 900,000 individual stores and outlets. Under a franchise system, such as McDonald's, an entrepreneur paid an initial franchise fee. The entrepreneur was then trained by McDonald's in its method of operating a restaurant, hiring employees, and other skills necessary to make the business successful. The entrepreneur was expected to pay as much as $1.8 million to McDonald's to open the restaurant.

In addition, the restaurant owner had to pay McDonald's a fee for advertising, as well as a percentage of monthly sales. In return, the owner could take advantage of the popular McDonald's brand name to help ensure that the restaurant would be successful. To make sure that the brand name was protected, the owner was expected to follow the company guidelines regarding signs for the store, colors for the exterior and interior, and store layout. In addition, the store owner had to use McDonald's food products and follow its methods for preparing meals. This ensured that customers would always receive the same quality food that they had come to expect from McDonald's.

The franchise system, although very popular, seemed to violate several elements of the Sherman Antitrust Act and the Clayton Act. For example, each franchisee was given a territory, and the franchisor agreed not to sell any other franchises in that particular area. This appeared to violate the Sherman Act because it involved an exclusive allocation of a market area to one business. As a result, competition was eliminated. In the *Addyston Pipe and Steel* case (1899), the Supreme Court had ruled that this activity was a violation of the Sherman Act.

Franchising also seemed to involve tying, a *per se* violation of the Sherman Act. The franchisee was expected to buy all of its products from the franchisor. This prevented the franchisee from shopping in the marketplace for a better price for the same products. It also prevented competitive suppliers from providing the products to the franchisee. In order to deal with these elements of franchising, the courts made a series of rulings in franchising cases from the 1960s to the 1980s, clarifying the Sherman Act.

SUSSER V. CARVEL CORPORATION

In 1965, a court of appeals in New York delivered its decision in *Susser* v. *Carvel Corp.* The case involved franchise owners of Carvel Ice Cream shops who had accused Carvel

Carvel Ice Cream stores were ubiquitous throughout the northeastern part of the United States during the mid-twentieth century. The company defeated a lawsuit aimed at forcing it to sell other brands besides Carvel in its own stores.

of violating the Sherman Antitrust Act. Specifically, Carvel was charged with price fixing, exclusive dealing, and tying— violations of the Sherman Act and the Clayton Act. According to the court documents, Carvel was a chain of franchises that had expanded from about 180 stores in 1954 to 400 stores by the early 1960s. These were located primarily in the eastern United States. The annual gross sales of the stores were as much as $8 million.

Under a 1955 agreement, Carvel required them to sell its products at prices fixed by the company and not to offer them at reduced sale prices. This was a clear case of vertical price fixing. However, Carvel had revised its requirements in 1957, issuing a new franchise agreement. This stated that "the dealer [franchise owner] shall have the right to sell Carvel's Frozen Dairy Product and/or other items authorized for sale by him under the terms of this agreement at any price that the dealer determines. Wherever Carvel recommends a retail price ... such recommendation is in no manner binding upon the dealer." The revised agreement had eliminated vertical price fixing by removing any required prices and only recommending them. This was not a violation of the antitrust laws, according to the Court of Appeals, at least in the area of price fixing.

With respect to exclusive dealing, the franchisees claimed that Carvel required them to sell only Carvel products. Under the 1955 agreement, these included the ice cream, as well as any containers for the ice cream, and other products, such as napkins. The requirement that franchisees purchase not only the ice cream but also the other products from Carvel was considered a tying arrangement under the antitrust laws. To get the ice cream, they had to agree to purchase everything else. However, as already mentioned, Carvel had revised the 1955 agreement in 1957. Under this agreement, the franchisees could purchase the non-ice cream products from any supplier. But they had to purchase all the ingredients for the ice cream from Carvel.

The appellate court ruled that the tying violation had been eliminated from the agreement. The franchisees could purchase, on the open market and at a competitive price, the non–ice cream items. However, the appeals court forcefully stated that Carvel was within its rights to insist that franchisees sell only the company's ice cream products. This was not considered exclusive dealing. "The fundamental device in the Carvel franchise agreement," said the chief judge in the appellate court, "is the licensing to the individual dealer of the right to employ the Carvel name in his advertising displays, on the products he sells, and on the store itself. The stores are uniform in design as well as in the public display.... The requirement that only Carvel products be sold at Carvel outlets derives from the desirability that the public identify each Carvel outlet as one of a chain which offers identical products at a uniform standard of quality."

In other words, Carvel stores were expected by its customers to sell only Carvel products. The sale of anything else might jeopardize the quality of the Carvel brand. By requiring the stores to sell only Carvel ice cream, the Carvel Company was not in violation of the Sherman Act. It was only protecting its name and the quality of its ice cream products.

SIEGEL V. CHICKEN DELIGHT

In 1971 an appeals court in California considered another franchising case. This one involved Harvey and Elaine Siegel, owners of a Chicken Delight franchise, as well as other franchisees. They were involved in a class action against Chicken Delight, a franchisor of restaurants. The franchise agreement required the Siegels and other owners to purchase only cooking equipment and packaging bearing the Chicken Delight trademark if they wanted to become franchise owners. The Siegels claimed that the packaging and equipment were being sold by Chicken Delight at prices that were higher than those being charged for the same products by other companies. This seemed like a case of illegal tying—being forced to buy a second product from a company.

In its consideration of the tying claims, the appeals court considered several issues. First, did the franchisees need to use only the equipment and packaging sold by Chicken Delight to maintain the quality of the product? The company claimed that the franchisees did have to use the equipment and packaging, and compared the situation to selling a left shoe without the right one. But the appeals court disagreed, saying, "it is apparent that the goodwill of the Chicken Delight trademark does not attach to the multitude of separate articles used in the operation of the licensed system or in the production of its end product." Therefore, Chicken Delight had violated the antitrust laws prohibiting tying.

The appellate court also considered another issue in making its decision. Under the Sherman Act a company had to possess demonstrated market power to impose tying. In other words, Chicken Delight had to control a large segment of the fast food chicken dinner business in its franchise. Only in this way could its requirement that franchisees purchase equipment from Chicken Delight significantly impact the business of other suppliers trying to sell the same equipment to the franchise owners. The appeals court ruled that Chicken Delight did control a large enough segment of the chicken dinner business to have this impact.

CONTINENTAL T.V., INC. V. GTE SYLVANIA INC.

In a 1977 case, the Supreme Court considered whether franchisors could restrict a franchisee to a specific location. This is a common element in franchise agreements. The case involved GTE Sylvania, a manufacturer of televisions, and

Defining Market Power

In *Siegel* v. *Chicken Delight*, the appeals court did not define how much of the market Chicken Delight had to control to significantly impact the business of competitive suppliers. In 1984, however, the Supreme Court more clearly defined what market power meant. In the case of *Jefferson Parish Hospital District No. 2* v. *Hyde*, the court stated that an amount above 30 percent was necessary for a per se violation of the Sherman Act. Currently, no franchisor controls that much of the market.

Continental, one of its distributors. Under Sylvania's franchise agreement during the 1960s, each distributor was permitted to sell televisions only at a stated location. When Continental wanted to open a second location where a distributor was already doing business, Sylvania said that this was not allowed under the franchise agreement without the company's permission. Nevertheless, Continental opened a store at the second location. As a result, Sylvania ended its relationship with the company, no longer permitting Continental to sell Sylvania television sets.

Continental claimed that Sylvania's actions were a *per se* violation of the Sherman Antitrust Act. It restricted a company to selling in only one area and prevented it from competing in another one. At the U.S. District Court level, Continental won the case and was awarded triple damages under the terms of the Clayton Act. Sylvania appealed and the case eventually reached the Supreme Court. Writing for the majority, Associate Justice Lewis Powell cited the "rule of reason." He stated that allocation of territories should not always be considered a violation of the Sherman Act. In some situations, it actually encourages competition. If a retailer is given an exclusive territory, it encourages him or her to enter the market and make the financial investment necessary to make a business succeed, Powell wrote. Therefore, the Supreme Court reversed the ruling of the appeals court.

NORMAN E. KREHL, ET AL., V. BASKIN-ROBBINS
In 1982, a court of appeals in California decided another important case that involved franchising. In this case, the owners of Baskin-Robbins ice cream stores brought a class action suit against the Baskin-Robbins Ice Cream Company (BRICO). The company operated a franchise system that

Baskin-Robbins ice cream stores, known for their dizzying number of flavors, sprang up all over the United States in the 1970s and 1980s. Here, Andy Pinero, 13, and his brother Isaiah, 9, eat Baskin-Robbins ice cream in Los Angeles.

included eight manufacturers of ice cream as well as the franchised store owners. In support of the franchisees, the company ran an extensive advertising campaign to publicize its ice cream products and encourage customers to buy them.

Among other things, the franchisees claimed that Baskin-Robbins had violated the tying provisions of the antitrust laws by requiring the store owners to purchase only the ice cream produced by the eight manufacturers. The appeals court, however, saw the situation differently. The judges ruled that the Baskin-Robbins trademark was "utterly dependent upon the perceived quality of the product it represents." In other words, the two could not be separated. In a tying case, however, there must be a tying product and a separate tied product. To obtain one a purchaser had to buy the other one. Here the ice cream and the trademark were one and the same product.

This case, the judges added, was different than *Chicken Delight*, in which the franchisees were required to buy products that had nothing to do with the quality of the chicken. In the *Baskin-Robbins* case, the ice cream had everything to do with the quality of the company trademark. Therefore, Baskin-Robbins had to insist that franchisees purchase the company's ice cream to safeguard the quality of the trademark in the minds of the customers.

The franchisees also accused Baskin-Robbins of practicing unlawful market allocation. In the *Addyston Pipe and Steel* case, separate companies decided between themselves which one of them would win a bid to provide pipe to a specific town or city. The Supreme Court had ruled that this was a violation of the Sherman Act. According to the franchisees, Baskin-Robbins carved out certain market areas for each ice cream manufacturer. But the appeals court found that, unlike earlier cases, Baskin-Robbins and its franchised manufacturers were not separate companies. BRICO had made all the decisions on its own as a single manufacturer. "When a manufacturer acts on its own, in pursuing its own market strategy, it is seeking to compete with other manufacturers by imposing what may be defended as reasonable" policies. Thus, the company had not violated the Sherman Act.

CHAPTER SEVEN

Boycotts
and Mergers

Any company can refuse to sell its products to another one. This is not prohibited under the Sherman Act. But suppose a group of well-known appliance companies get together and refuse to deal with a store that sells televisions and kitchen equipment. Instead, the suppliers decide to deal with another store, located right next door, which is part of a large chain. The chain gives the suppliers far more business and wants them not to sell to its competitor. This is exactly what happened in San Francisco, California, in the 1950s. The suppliers refused to sell their products to an appliance store named Klor's and instead dealt only with its competitor, the Broadway-Hale Stores. The Supreme Court held that this was a boycott against Klor's—a restraint of trade and competition that violates the Sherman Antitrust Act.

As the Court stated in *Klor's, Inc.* v. *Broadway-Hale Stores, Inc.,* in 1959, "Group boycotts, or concerted refusals by traders to deal with other traders, have long been held to be in the forbidden category [under the Sherman Act]." In other words, this was a *per se* violation of the Sherman Antitrust Act and the appliance suppliers had to stop what they had been doing. This would be enforced by the courts.

Group boycotts occur not only among retailers and their suppliers but also in other business areas, such as professional sports. One case of a boycott involved professional basketball player Spencer Haywood. Born in Mississippi in 1949, Haywood and his family moved to Detroit when he was in high school. There, Haywood played for Pershing High School and helped his team win a state championship. After graduation he went to Trinidad State Junior College in Colorado, where he was a standout player averaging more than twenty-eight points per game. Haywood's exceptional skills earned him a place on the U. S. Olympic basketball team in 1968, leading the team to a gold medal by shooting more than sixteen points per game.

After spending a year at the University of Detroit, Haywood turned professional, joining the Denver Rockets of the American Basketball Association. As a result of his outstanding performance, he was named Rookie of the Year in the 1969–1970 season. Haywood then left the Rockets and signed a contract with the Seattle SuperSonics in the National Basketball Association (NBA). However, the NBA had a rule that barred any player from joining the league until four years after completing high school. Haywood decided to challenge the rule, claiming that the NBA teams were participating in a group boycott, a *per se* violation of the Sherman Antitrust Act.

The U.S. District Court in California agreed with Haywood. The court stated, "If Haywood is unable to continue to play professional basketball for Seattle, he will suffer irreparable

Basketball superstar Spencer Haywood (*right*) successfully challenged the NBA rule barring any player from joining their league until he had been out of high school for four years.

injury in that a substantial part of his playing career will have been [lost], his physical condition, skills and coordination will deteriorate from lack of high-level competition, his public acceptance as a superstar will diminish to the detriment of his career, his self-esteem and his pride will have been injured, and a great injustice will be perpetrated on him." The court granted Haywood an injunction—that is, it stopped the action of the NBA and allowed him to play for Seattle.

The NBA appealed the decision, which eventually reached the Supreme Court. In a majority decision, written by Associate Justice William O. Douglas in 1971, the Supreme Court upheld the ruling of the district court. This led to an agreement between Haywood and the NBA, permitting him to continue playing with the Seattle SuperSonics. The decision in *Haywood* v. *National Basketball Association* not only helped Haywood but other players, too. Basketball players such as LeBron James and Kobe Bryant were able to join the NBA directly from high school.

Another case of a group boycott involved an association of trial lawyers in Washington, D.C. The Superior Court Trial Lawyers Association (SCTLA) represented poor clients who were accused of committing crimes. In the 1980s, the lawyers in the association decided that they would no longer represent these clients unless their legal fees were increased. The Federal Trade Commission investigated the case and found that the SCTLA was trying to fix prices and boycott the D.C. legal system—both violations of the antitrust laws. The Federal Court of Appeals agreed. But the court also stated that the SCTLA was trying to communicate a "political message to the public," so citizens would put pressure on the government to raise the legal fees of the association's lawyers. The Court added that this right was protected under the First

Amendment to the U.S. Constitution, which guaranteed freedom of speech.

The U.S. Supreme Court saw the case differently. In *Federal Trade Commission v. Superior Court Trial Lawyers Association,* Associate Justice John Paul Stevens delivered the majority decision of the court in 1990. Stevens called the action by SCTLA a boycott and "a naked restraint of price . . . in violation of the antitrust laws."

In 1991 the Supreme Court decided another group boycott case. This case involved an eye doctor named Simon J. Pinhas. Dr. Pinhas claimed that Summit Health, which owned nineteen hospitals, and Midway Hospital Medical Center in Los Angeles, California (owned by Summit), had conspired to ruin his medical practice. Summit and Midway dealt with patients from outside California, so the case involved interstate commerce.

In this case, Medicare—a federal health program for elderly patients—had decided to change its coverage for eye surgery. In the past, Medicare had paid for a physician and an assistant to perform the surgery. But in 1986, Medicare stopped this practice, saying that it would no longer pay physicians for the cost of an assistant. Dr. Pinhas asked Midway to stop requiring both a physician and an assistant at eye surgery. However, the hospital refused. Instead, Pinhas was expected to pay for the assistant himself. When Pinhas refused to agree, he was suspended from Midway Hospital and could no longer perform surgery there.

Pinhas sued Midway and Summit, charging that they were involved in a group boycott preventing him from practicing medicine. He lost his case at the U.S. District Court level, because he was unable to prove that his dismissal from the hospital affected interstate commerce. However, the decision

Per Se v. the

The Supreme Court had ruled in the *Klor's* and *Haywood* cases that boycotts were a *per se* violation of the Sherman Act. But in a later case, the justices changed their minds. This case involved a group of about one hundred retail stationers who sold office supplies in the Pacific Northwest in the 1950s. They had joined together to form a buying cooperative, Northwest Wholesale Stationers, that purchased items in bulk and at lower prices than if each store had bought them individually. The cooperative provided warehouse space to store the supplies. And, at the end of each year, if the cooperative made a profit, each retail stationer shared in it, receiving a rebate on the cost of its purchases from the cooperative.

Since the 1950s, Pacific Stationery and Printing Company, a large retailer, had been a member of the cooperative. Pacific sold office supplies as a retailer and a wholesaler. In 1974, the cooperative changed its regulations, preventing any member from being a wholesaler. However, an exception was made for Pacific, which had been a member for so many years. Shortly afterward, in 1977, Pacific was sold to new owners, but they did not inform the cooperative of the change in ownership. As a result, the members of the cooperative voted to end Pacific's membership in the group.

Pacific Stationery sued the cooperative in the U. S. District Court in Oregon, charging its members with a group boycott. The court found that expelling Pacific had not affected its ability to compete against the other members. The court applied the "rule of reason" to the case, stating that Northwest had not violated the Sherman Act. The case was eventually appealed to the U.S. Supreme Court, where the

Rule of Reason

majority decision was delivered in 1985 by Associate Justice William Brennan.

In *Northwest Wholesale Stationers, Inc.* v. *Pacific Stationery and Printing Co.*, Justice Brennan recognized that group boycotts were usually per se violations of the Sherman Act, citing the case of *Klor's, Inc.* v. *Broadway-Hale Stores, Inc.* But he added that in that and similar cases, "the boycott often cut off access to a supply [of goods], facility, or market necessary to enable the boycotted firm to compete. . . ." But, he added, that had not happened in the *Pacific Stationery* case. In addition, the cooperative may have acted properly by expelling Pacific. Northwest needed to know the names of the new owners to ensure their credit was sound and they could pay for supplies purchased from the cooperative.

was reversed in a court of appeals. The appeals court stated that Pinhas did not need to prove that the decision by Midway and Summit would specifically affect him. He only had to show that if a similar decision were made regarding other doctors and they were also dismissed, it would have an impact on the number of patients coming to the hospital from other states. Summit then appealed the decision to the Supreme Court.

In a 5 to 4 decision, delivered in 1991, the Supreme Court ruled in favor of Pinhas. In *Summit Health, Ltd.* v. *Pinhas,* Associate Justice John Paul Stevens wrote the opinion for the majority. He stated that Summit was clearly involved in interstate commerce because services by ophthalmologists were regularly performed for out-of-state patients. Then Stevens went on to look at the impact on other ophthalmologists if Summit treated them the same way that they had dealt with Dr. Pinhas. They would have been fired just as Dr. Pinhas had been fired. As a result, Stevens believed that an effort—a conspiracy—would have existed by the hospital to fire all the ophthalmologists.

This would have impacted the hospital's ability to serve ophthalmology patients from out of state. "A conspiracy to eliminate the entire ophthalmological department of the hospital, like a conspiracy to destroy the hospital itself, would unquestionably affect interstate commerce . . . ," Justice Stevens wrote. Stevens also emphasized that the action against the other doctors need not actually occur, but that the issue was "the potential harm that would ensue if the conspiracy were successful." Under the Sherman Act, not only the impact of a group boycott itself, but also the potential effect if the boycott occurred some time in the future, was considered illegal.

MERGERS AND THE ANTITRUST LAWS

The Clayton Act, passed in 1914, spelled out the Sherman Act in more specific language. Section 7 of the Clayton Act states that no company involved in interstate commerce can acquire another company through the purchase of its stock if "the effect of such acquisition may be substantially to lessen competition, or tend to create a monopoly."

The Clayton Act is not designed to prevent mergers—the acquisition of one company by another—if the mergers do not reduce competition or lead to a monopoly. Rather, the Clayton Act is aimed at preventing any company from dominating a market. For example, suppose four large firms control 75 percent of a specific market, such as the sale of men's and women's shoes. The federal government may oppose the merger of one of these large firms with a much smaller firm, even if the merger results in as little as a 2 percent increase in market share for the merged firms. This may be defined as "substantially to lessen competition." In 1950, the Celler–Kefauver Act amended the Clayton Act. This new law stated that not only the acquisition of another firm's stock as part of a merger but also acquisition of its physical assets—products—was illegal if it tended to create a monopoly.

In its examination of mergers, the government looks at various issues. One of these is the product market, such as shoes. Another issue is the geographical market. This may be a national market for shoes, or a regional market, such as the northeastern or southwestern states. A third issue is the concentration—how much of the market is controlled by the merged firms.

One of the most famous merger cases involved two shoe companies, Brown Shoe and G. R. Kinney. In terms of sales, Brown was America's third biggest retailer, with more than

When the Brown Shoe and G. R. Kinney companies proposed a merger, they were prevented from doing so by the federal government, under the provisions of the Clayton Act.

1,200 stores in the mid–1950s. Kinney was the eighth largest with 350 stores. In 1955, the two companies proposed a
merger, but the decision was opposed by the federal government under Section 7 of the Clayton Act. The case was tried
in the lower courts and eventually reached the Supreme
Court, where a decision was handed down in 1962. In *Brown
Shoe Co., Inc.* v. *United States,* the Court looked at the various
cities where both companies had shoe stores. It noted that in
some cities, their combined share of the women's shoe market ranged from 33 percent to 57 percent.

The majority of the Supreme Court concluded that "the
merger spurred an increasing trend toward concentration
in the shoe industry," and should be enjoined [prevented].
In other words, the Court was not only concerned about the
impact of this specific merger but also its possible effect on
the shoe industry in the future, where greater concentration
might occur, restricting competition.

A year later, the Court reached a similar conclusion in
United States v. *Philadelphia National Bank.* Philadelphia
National Bank wanted to merge with Girard Trust Corn
Exchange Bank. This would have created a single bank in the
Philadelphia area with 36 percent of total assets and deposits. The banks said that the merger would enable them to
increase the amount of money they could loan and compete
with large banks from New York that were trying to expand
their business into Philadelphia. The Supreme Court saw the
situation quite differently. The Court said that the means—
competing with out-of-state banks—did not justify the ends.
The means were a violation of the Sherman Act.

Another merger case involved two large supermarket
chains—American Stores Co., and Lucky Stores, Inc. In the
1980s, American had approximately 1,500 stores in forty

states, while Lucky owned 340 stores in seven states. When the companies decided to merge, California filed a lawsuit to stop the merger. American owned 252 stores in California, and the state government feared that a merger with Lucky— the largest supermarket chain in the state—would undermine competition. The state sued under the Sherman Act and the Clayton Act, charging that the merger would eliminate competition in many relevant geographic markets.

The U.S. District Court in California agreed to prevent the merger, saying that the state had convinced the court that "Californians will be irreparably harmed if the proposed merger is completed." American appealed the decision to the U.S. Supreme Court. In 1990, Associate Justice John Paul Stevens wrote the decision for the 9 to 0 majority in *California* v. *American Stores Co.*, upholding the decision of the lower court.

MERGERS IN THE 1990s

In 1992, Democrat Bill Clinton was elected president. Under President Clinton, the Antitrust Division of the Justice Department, as well as the FTC, closely examined a number of proposed mergers to determine if they violated the Sherman and Clayton Acts. In 1997, for example, the FTC asked the courts for an injunction to stop the merger of Staples and Office Depot, two of the largest discount office supply companies. Looking at the geographic areas affected by the merger, economists for the commission produced evidence that showed prices for office supplies were lower in cities where both companies ran independent stores. Looking at the market, the FTC also pointed out that the two companies together would control 75 percent of sales in the office supply superstore market. The federal district court in

Exceptions to the Clayton Law

Sometimes, the Supreme Court makes exceptions to mergers and how they relate to the Clayton Act. For example, suppose a company is doing poorly and about to go out of business. Only one other company in the same field is willing to acquire the failing firm. Under the Failing Company Doctrine, the Supreme Court may allow this merger to go forward rather than let the failing company go out of business.

In 1974, the Supreme Court considered the case of *United States* v. *General Dynamics Corp.* At this point, General Dynamics had acquired several struggling coal companies, making it America's fifth-biggest coal producer. In a majority decision written by Associate Justice Potter Stewart, the court decided not to oppose these acquisitions, although competition was being reduced in the coal industry. Justice Stewart looked at other factors, including the declining coal business across the United States. He also mentioned the fact that at least one of the companies acquired by General Dynamics would have been unable to remain competitive in the coal industry in the future. Therefore, the acquisition would not have a negative impact on competition.

Washington, D.C., agreed, granted the injunction, and the merger was stopped.

In 1998, the Justice Department decided to stop the acquisition of Northrop Grumman by Lockheed Martin. These were two of the largest defense contractors in the United States. The Justice Department stated that the merger would result in "higher prices and lower quality in advanced tactical and strategic aircraft, airborne early warning radar systems, sonar systems and several types of countermeasures systems that save our pilots from being shot down when they are flying in hostile skies." In other words, the merger would greatly reduce competition and lead to higher prices, a violation of the antitrust acts. As a result, it was stopped.

That same year, the Clinton Administration brought its most important antitrust case yet—the case against computer software company Microsoft.

CHAPTER EIGHT

Recent
Antitrust Cases

In 1998, the Microsoft case came before the U.S. District Court in Washington, D.C. Presiding over the court was Judge Thomas Penfield Jackson, and the case that had come before him was *United States* v. *Microsoft.*

Microsoft, the huge computer software company, controlled about 85 percent of the operating systems for personal computers through its Microsoft Windows software product. Under the Sherman Act, not every monopoly was illegal. Microsoft was being sued by the U.S. Department of Justice and twenty states for maintaining this monopoly in ways that violated the Sherman Act. Specifically, the charges involved the company's efforts to persuade its customers—computer equipment manufacturers, Internet access providers, and others—to use the company's Internet browser, Internet Explorer. At the same time, these customers were expected to refuse to use a rival browser, Netscape, which controlled 90 percent of the browser market because of its

Bill Gates grew Microsoft from a start-up in his bedroom into a software company so large that, by the 1990s, it controlled about 85 percent of the computer operating systems in the United States. Here, James Bartlesdale of Netscape talks to reporters after testifying against Microsoft in U.S. District Court.

highly effective software. Some of the methods that Microsoft was alleged to have used to drive out Netscape were tying, refusals to deal with customers, and exclusionary contracts—all violations of the Sherman Act.

Leading the case for the Justice Department were Joel Klein, deputy chief of the antitrust division, and David Boies, considered one of America's leading trial lawyers. Boies was called an "eccentric genius" by some of his colleagues, who said that he had the ability to cut through large quantities of information to get to the heart of a case. Leading the team of lawyers defending Microsoft was William Neukom. The government's case rested heavily on approximately 30 million documents, many of them e-mails.

These had been turned over by Microsoft in response to investigative demands from the Justice Department. These demands are similar to subpoenas that require an individual to testify or turn over evidence.

After reading stacks of these e-mails, Boies commented that the harsh language used by Microsoft and the way it treated other companies came "almost from a different era in terms of business conduct." Based on these documents, the government contended that Microsoft's unlawful methods were designed to drive Netscape Navigator out of the Internet browser business. Microsoft wanted to control the browser industry. In addition, according to the *New York Times*, "What frightened Microsoft was that [Netscape] Navigator could also be used as a 'platform,' a layer of software on which other programs can run. This is the main function of an operating system, a market in which Microsoft has a monopoly with Windows."

The e-mails produced by Boies and his team included a message from Bill Gates, then president of Microsoft. The company had been producing an operating system designed to support Apple's Macintosh computers. But Apple had decided to offer the Netscape Navigator as part of its package to its customers. Gates wrote to members of his staff, "[We] need a way to push these guys and [threatening to cancel Mac Office] is the only one that seems to make them move." Gates then added that he had called Apple and threatened to cancel the Mac Office. As a result, Apple agreed to offer Internet Explorer—Microsoft's browser—with the Mac and not to install Navigator on the Mac's hard drive, or computer system.

This type of exclusive dealing was a violation of the Sherman Act because it restricted Netscape's ability to do business in the Internet browser market. Since Microsoft had so much control of the operating system market, it could use its legal monopoly to force customers to stop dealing with Netscape and make an exclusive deal to use Microsoft's Internet Explorer.

In another e-mail, James Allchin, a senior Microsoft executive, stated in 1997: "I do not believe we can win on our current path. Even if we get Internet Explorer totally competitive with Navigator, why would we be chosen? They have 80 percent market share. My conclusion is we have to leverage Windows more." Allchin appeared as a witness during the trial, and Judge Jackson asked him what the e-mail meant. Allchin said that he meant "There's a great opportunity and, boy, we shouldn't miss it." But Jackson recalled later, "When Allchin told me that 'leverage' simply meant use it as an opportunity, that was not credible."

Instead, "leverage" seemed to mean making deals like the one with Apple. Court documents also revealed that Microsoft had agreed to promote the products of large companies that provided customers with Internet access services in return for promoting and distributing Internet Explorer and not offering Netscape. In addition, Microsoft offered rebates and other payments to Internet access providers whenever they upgraded customers to new software if it included Internet Explorer instead of Netscape.

During the trial, Steven McGeady, a vice president of Intel—a major manufacturer of microprocessors, the electronic brain for computers—testified that Microsoft said it would not support Intel's new products if it offered them with Netscape as the Internet browser. "It was clear to us that the threat was credible and fairly terrifying," McGeady added. This refusal to deal with Intel unless it made an exclusionary arrangement with Microsoft was a violation of the Sherman Act.

America Online (AOL), which was a leading Internet service provider in the 1990s, had a similar experience with Microsoft. Recalling a meeting with Bill Gates, an AOL executive wrote to others in the company, "Gates delivered a characteristically blunt query: 'How much do we need to pay you?' he asked, "to screw Netscape.' " Instead of money, Microsoft agreed in 1996 to let AOL offer a link to Microsoft Office in return for an agreement by AOL to provide Internet Explorer to more than 85 percent of its subscribers. This was another example of exclusive dealing.

Another way that Microsoft hoped to defeat Netscape, according to Allchin, was "Windows integration." This meant combining Internet Explorer with Microsoft Office, so a customer who bought Windows automatically got Internet Explorer. The Justice Department claimed that this was an example of tying—a violation of the Sherman Act. Microsoft, however, contended that the browser was so completely connected with the Windows software that the two could not be sold independently without harming the entire system.

During the trial, the Justice Department produced a witness who separated Internet Explorer from Microsoft Windows and showed that they could run independently. In response, Microsoft's attorneys produced a videotape in which company employees tried to separate Windows from Internet Explorer and demonstrated that it damaged the Windows software system. Since the two were completely bound together, the lawyers said, a customer who bought Windows was not being forced to buy a separate program—tying—but purchased only one system with two different components.

Lawyers for Microsoft and the federal government also argued over the company's use of its monopoly powers in pricing. A key issue was whether Microsoft substantially raised prices, thus causing harm to consumers. The company produced evidence showing that it had charged low prices for Windows, which amounted to less than 5 percent of the price of a personal computer. In response the government produced Microsoft e-mails showing that Windows prices had risen from about $19 for the software package in 1990 to more than $49 in 1996. Meanwhile, the prices of other computer parts had declined, indicating that Microsoft had been charging too much and harming consumers.

However, Microsoft contended that it had made Windows into a leading software system by consistently doing research that improved the product and made it the best in the field. This was the only way that Microsoft could remain a leader in technology, a field that was constantly changing with new products and innovations. The research and development was costly and had to be reflected, at least to some degree, in the price. Nevertheless, the company's lawyers emphasized that Microsoft did not raise prices to harm consumers. Instead it offered Internet Explorer as a free part of Windows.

Testifying for Microsoft, Richard L. Schmalensee, an economist and dean of the Massachusetts Institute of Technology's Sloan School of Management, said, "Microsoft is constantly concerned with being displaced as a leader." In other words, it was not a true monopoly and had to offer competitive prices and products to remain a leading software company.

After listening to months of testimony, Judge Jackson finally handed down his decision in April 2000. He found that Microsoft had violated antitrust law through its anticompetitive actions and had also tried to gain a monopoly in the browser market. The judge wrote that "Microsoft maintained its monopoly power by anticompetitive means and attempted to monopolize the Web browser market unlawfully tying its Web browser to its operating system." Judge Jackson also called for Microsoft to be broken up into separate companies—one offering its Windows operating system, and the other offering the rest of its products, such as Internet Explorer. Nearly ninety years earlier, a similar decision had been made regarding Standard Oil.

The order to break up the company was delayed, as Microsoft appealed the decision to the U.S. Court of Appeals. In a decision handed down in 2001, the appeals court agreed with Judge Jackson regarding some of Microsoft's anticompetitive behavior. But it did not agree that Microsoft had tried to gain a monopoly in the browser market, nor did the appeals court find enough evidence to support a tying violation of the Sherman Act. As a result, the appeals court stated that there was no reason to break up Microsoft into separate companies, especially since this would result in a loss of the company's efficiency in the marketplace.

Meanwhile, AOL had purchased Netscape and filed a lawsuit against Microsoft for damaging the Navigator product. The two companies settled in 2003, with Microsoft paying AOL $750 million and giving the company permission to distribute Internet Explorer for free for seven years. By this time

Internet Explorer had become a very popular browser, and Netscape's share of the Internet browser market gradually dropped to almost zero because it was unable to compete with Microsoft's browser and its superior financial resources.

ANTITRUST CASES IN THE TWENTY-FIRST CENTURY

The opinions in the Microsoft antitrust case were among the most important of the early twenty-first century. Over the next eight years, the Republican administration of President George W. Bush took a different approach to antitrust than the Clinton Administration. As *New York Times* reporter Stephen Labaton said, it was "the most relaxed and least aggressive approach since the last years of the [Ronald] Reagan presidency" in the late 1980s. Labaton referred specifically to a decision by the Justice Department to approve an effort by Whirlpool—a large appliance manufacturer—to acquire Maytag. The new company would control about 75 percent of the home appliance market. Nevertheless, the Justice Department did not challenge the acquisition.

In part, this was because the government decided to define the market very broadly. It was defined as not just U.S. home appliances and appliance makers, but as foreign appliance makers as well. This meant that the new company had a much smaller share of the market. Labaton added that "no one can remember a major case under the Sherman Antitrust Act against a company for acting as a monopolist since the Clinton administration's pursuit of Microsoft." The Bush Administration believed that the federal government should use as little regulation of the marketplace as possible.

Nevertheless, several important antitrust cases did reach the Supreme Court. In 2004, Associate Justice Anthony Kennedy wrote a 9 to 0 majority decision in *United States Postal Service* v. *Flamingo Industries*. The case involved the United States Postal Service (USPS), which was sued by Flamingo Industries, a manufacturer of mail sacks for the postal service. Flamingo's contract with USPS was ended by the postal service and an exclusive contract to manufacture the postal sacks was awarded to a foreign company. Flamingo sued USPS, charging that the postal service had given a monopoly for making the mail sacks to the new company.

Justice Kennedy pointed out that the Sherman Act stated that only a "person" could be sued under the terms of the act. The Sherman Act defined a person as a corporation or association "authorized by the laws of either the United States [or of States or foreign governments]." Kennedy added that the USPS is not a corporation or association but a part of the executive branch of the U.S. government. In earlier cases, the Court had ruled that the U.S. government is not a person. Any part of the government is therefore not considered a person under the Sherman Act. As a result, the USPS could not be sued under the act.

In 2007, the Supreme Court heard another important antitrust case, *Leegin Creative Leather Products, Inc.* v. *PSKS, Inc.* This case involved a policy by Leegin, a maker of women's fashion products, to require retailers who sold these products to charge nothing less than a minimum price fixed by the company. Since the 1911 case of *Dr. Miles Medical Co.* v. *John D. Park and Sons Co.*, this practice—called vertical minimum price agreements—had been a *per se* violation of the Sherman Act. When PSKS, a retailer, decided to sell Leegin products below the minimum price, Leegin refused to deal with the retailer.

Judges generally abide by the legal principle known as

The probusiness Bush administration kept its hands off large corporations, largely ignoring the Sherman Antitrust Act. The Obama administration has said it would reverse that direction, but it did not seem to be an immediate priority.

stare decisis, which means following the precedents set in earlier decisions. But in a 5 to 4 decision, the Supreme Court decided to overturn the *Dr. Miles* case. Justice Anthony Kennedy wrote the majority opinion in the case. Kennedy said that these practices should be judged by the rule of reason.

Kennedy added that Leegin's policy of minimum prices was

not anticompetitive but improved competition. With minimum pricing, retailers no longer would try to undercut each other in their sales of Leegin brand products, but instead would concentrate on competing against other brands. As Kennedy wrote, the "primary purpose [of antitrust laws] is to protect interbrand competition [between rival brands]." The court decided that the minimum pricing encouraged competition, instead of discouraging it. Therefore, it was not a violation of the Sherman Act.

Under the administration of President Barack Obama, who took office in 2009, the Justice Department has announced that it would proceed against agribusiness firms under the Sherman Act. There are a few large firms that have a near monopoly over food production and seed manufacture, threatening to stifle competition.

Throughout its history, the Sherman Antitrust Act has been interpreted differently as the justices on the Supreme Court have changed. The Supreme Court has also disagreed with lower courts and their interpretation of the Sherman Act.

Over more than a century since its enactment and after hundreds of cases, the meaning of the Sherman Act continues to evolve. The legislators who designed the Sherman Act could not have envisioned that their legislation would impact future generations of PC users. Nevertheless, the continued strength of the law demonstrates its importance and timelessness in twenty-first century America.

Glossary

horizontal integration—Control by one company of all competitors in an industry.

horizontal price fixing—Controlling prices across an industry.

interstate commerce—Business conducted across state lines.

monopoly—An organization that controls at least 75 to 80 percent of a market.

***per se* violation**—An activity that is always considered a violation *per se—by itself*—of the Sherman Act.

stare decisis—The legal principle by which a court respects precedents set by earlier opinions.

trust—Another term for a monopoly.

tying—Forcing a company that buys one product to also purchase another, often inferior, product.

vertical integration—The control of every aspect of a business from raw materials to finished product to method of bringing the product to market.

vertical price fixing—Controlling prices at every level of sale, from wholesale to retail.

Chronology

1890	Sherman Antitrust Act is passed
1895	*United States v. E. C. Knight Co.*
1897	*United States v. Trans-Missouri Freight Association*
1899	*Addyston Pipe and Steel Co. v. United States*
1901	Theodore Roosevelt becomes president after President McKinley is assassinated
1903	Elkins Act passed, outlawing railroad rebates
1904	*Northern Securities Co. v. United States*
1905	*Swift and Co. v. United States*
1908	William Howard Taft is elected president
1911	*Standard Oil of New Jersey Co. v. United States* *Dr. Miles Medical Co. v. John D. Park & Sons Co.* case is decided by Supreme Court
1912	Woodrow Wilson is elected president
1914	Clayton Antitrust Act is passed Federal Trade Commission Act is passed

1922   *Federal Baseball Club of Baltimore v. National League of Professional Baseball Clubs*

1927   *United States v. Trenton Potteries Company*

1929   Great Depression begins

1932   Franklin Roosevelt is elected president

1933   *Appalachian Coals, Inc. v. United States*

1935   National Labor Relations Act is passed

1940   *Apex Hosiery Co. v. Leader*

1941   *United States v. Hutcheson*

1947   *International Salt Co. v. United States*

1948   *United States v. Paramount Pictures, Inc.*

1953   *Toolson v. New York Yankees*

1956   *United States v. E. I. DuPont Nemours & Co.*

1957   *Radovich v. National Football League*
               Kansas City Star Company v. United States

1960   *United States v. Parke, Davis and Co.*

1962   *Brown Shoe Co., Inc. v. United States*

1963 *United States* v. *Philadelphia National Bank*

1965 *Susser* v. *Carvel Corp.*

1966 *United States* v. *General Motors Corp.*

1971 *Siegel* v. *Chicken Delight*
      Haywood v. *National Basketball Association*

1972 *Flood* v. *Kuhn*

1974 *United States* v. *General Dynamics Corp.*

1977 *Continental T.V., Inc.* v. *GTE Sylvania Inc.*

1982 *Norman E. Krehl, et al.* v. *Baskin-Robbins*

1985 *Northwest Wholesale Stationers, Inc.* v. *Pacific
      Stationery and Printing Co.*

1990 *Federal Trade Commission* v. *Superior Court Trial
      Lawyers Association*
      California v. *American Stores Co.*

1991 *Summit Health, Ltd.* v. *Pinhas*

1998 *United States* v. *Microsoft*

2004 *United States Postal Service* v. *Flamingo Industries*

2007 *Leegin Creative Leather Products, Inc.* v. *PSKS, Inc.*

From Bill to Law

For a proposal to become a federal law, it must go through many steps:

In Congress:

1. A bill is proposed by a citizen, a legislator, the president, or another interested party. Most bills originate in the House and then are considered in the Senate.

2. A representative submits the bill to the House (the first reading). A senator submits it to the Senate. The person (or people) who introduces the bill is its main sponsor. Other lawmakers can become sponsors to show support for the bill. Each bill is read three times before the House or the Senate.

3. The bill is assigned a number and referred to the committee(s) and subcommittee(s) dealing with the topic. Each committee adopts its own rules, following guidelines of the House and the Senate. The committee chair controls scheduling for the bill.

4. The committees hold hearings if the bill is controversial or complex. Experts and members of the public may testify. Congress may compel witnesses to testify if they do not do so voluntarily.

5. The committee reviews the bill, discusses it, adds amendments, and makes other changes it deems necessary during markup sessions.

6. The committee votes on whether to support the bill, oppose it, or take no action on it and issues a report on its findings and recommendations.

7. A bill that receives a favorable committee report goes to the Rules Committee to be scheduled for consideration by the full House or Senate.

8. If the committee delays a bill or if the Rules Committee fails to schedule it, House members can sign a discharge motion and call for a vote on the matter. If a majority votes to release the bill from committee, it is scheduled on the calendar as any other bill would be. Senators may vote to discharge the bill from a committee as well. More commonly, though, a senator will add the bill as an amendment to an unrelated bill in order to get it past the committee blocking it. Or a senator can request that a bill be put directly on the Senate calendar, where it will be scheduled for debate. House and Senate members can also vote to suspend the rules and vote directly on a bill. Bills passed in this way must receive support from two thirds of those voting.

9. Members of both houses debate the bill. In the House, a chairperson moderates the discussion and each speaker's time is limited. Senators can speak on the issue for as long as they wish. Senators who want to block the bill may debate for hours in a tactic known as a filibuster. A three-fifths vote of the Senate is required to stop the filibuster (cloture), and talk on the bill is then limited to one hour per senator.

10. Following the debate, the bill is read section by section (the second reading). Members may propose amendments, which are voted on before the final bill comes up for a vote.

11. The full House and Senate then debate the entire bill and those amendments approved previously. Debate continues until a majority of members vote to "move the previous question" or approve a special resolution forcing a vote.

12. A full quorum—at least 218 members in the House, 51 in the Senate—must be present for a vote to be held. A member may request a formal count of members to ensure a quorum is on hand. Absent members are sought when there is no quorum.

13. Before final passage, opponents are given a last chance to propose amendments that alter the bill; the members vote on them.

14. A bill needs approval from a majority of those voting to pass. Members who do not want to take a stand on the issue may choose to abstain (not vote at all) or merely vote present.

15. If the House passes the bill, it goes on to the Senate. By that time, bills often have more than one hundred amendments attached to them. Occasionally, a Senate bill will go to the House.

16. If the bill passes in the same form in both the House and the Senate, it is sent to the clerk to be recorded.

17. If the Senate and the House version differ, the Senate sends the bill to the House with the request that members approve the changes.

18. If the two houses disagree on the changes, the bill may go to conference, where members appointed by the House and the Senate work out a compromise if possible.

19. The House and the Senate vote on the revised bill agreed to in conference. Further amendments may be added and the process repeated if the Senate and the House version of the bill differ.

20. The bill goes to the president for a signature.

To the President:

1. If the president signs the bill, it becomes law.

2. If the president vetoes the bill, it goes back to Congress, which can override his veto with a two-thirds vote in both houses.

3. If the president takes no action, the bill automatically becomes law after ten days if Congress is still in session.

4. If Congress adjourns and the president has taken no action on the bill within ten days, it does not become law. This is known as a pocket veto.

The time from introduction of the bill to the signing can range from several months to the entire two-year session. If a bill does not win approval during the session, it can be reintroduced in the next Congress, where it will have to go through the whole process again.

Notes

Chapter 1

p. 9, "The time was ripe . . .": *The Life History of the United States: Steel and Steam* (New York: Time-Life Books, 1975), 134.

p. 9, "Standard Oil, for example . . .": "The Dismantling of the Standard Oil Trust," *Linux Information Project,* 2008, www.linfo.org/standardoil.html (accessed on November 7, 2008).

p. 10, "During that period . . .": Allan Nevins and Henry Steele Commager, *A Pocket History of the United States* (New York: Pocket Books, 1992), 256.

p. 12, "Between 1870 and 1900 . . ." Allan Nevins and Henry Steele Commager, *A Pocket History of the United States* (New York: Pocket Books, 1992), 261.

p. 12, "This is a Senate . . .": *The Life History of the United States,* 126.

p. 12, "William Avery Rockefeller . . .": Keith Poole, "People and Events: John D. Rockefeller Senior, 1839–1937," *American Experience,* 2000, www.pbs.org/wgbh/amex/rockefellers/peopleevents/p_rock_jsr.html (accessed on November 7, 2008).

p. 14, "Soon afterward, he went . . ." Keith Poole, "People and Events: John D. Rockefeller Senior, 1839–1937," *American Experience,* 2000, www.pbs.org/wgbh/amex/rockefellers/peopleevents/p_rock_jsr.html (accessed on November 7, 2008).

p. 14, " According to historian Keith Poole . . ." Keith Poole, "People and Events: John D. Rockefeller Senior, 1839–1937,"

American Experience, 2000, www.pbs.org/wgbh/amex/
rockefellers/peopleevents/p_rock_jsr.html (accessed on
November 7, 2008).

p. 15, "According to historian Ron Chernow...": Ron Chernow,
Titan: The Life of John D. Rockefeller Sr. (New York: Random
House, 1998), Book Reviews, http://eh.net/book reviews/
library/0373 (accessed on November 10, 2008).

p. 15, "Later some owners . . .": Keith Poole, "People and
Events: John D. Rockefeller Senior, 1839–1937," *American
Experience,* 2000, www.pbs.org/wgbh/amex/rockefellers/
peopleevents/p_rock_jsr.html (accessed on November 7,
2008).

p. 15, "Meanwhile, on the retail...": Keith Poole, "People and
Events: John D. Rockefeller Senior, 1839–1937," *American
Experience,* 2000, www.pbs.org/wgbh/amex/rockefellers/
peopleevents/p_rock_jsr.html (accessed on November 7,
2008).

p. 15, "Samuel Dodd, a lawyer...": "People and Events: John D.
Rockefeller Senior, 1839–1937," *American Experience,* 2000,
www.pbs.org/wgbh/amex/rockefellers/peopleevents/p_
rock_jsr.html (accessed on November 7, 2008).

p. 16, "Standard also succeeded in . . ." *Titan,* 258,

p. 16, "During the 1870s . . .": *Pocket History of the United
States,* 326.

p. 17, "all chartered monopolies . . .": William Letwin, *Law
and Economic Policy in America: The Evolution of the Sherman Antitrust Act* (Chicago: University of Chicago Press,
1981), 67.

p. 17, "Their great business capacity . . .": "A Great Monopoly," *Atlantic,* December 10, 1999, www.theatlantic.com/
doc/print/199911u/monopoly (accessed on November 10,
2008).

p. 18, "monster business establishments . . .": *Law and Economic Policy,* 68–69.

p. 18, "While we recognize . . .": *Law and Economic Policy,* 85.

p. 18, "The paramount issues . . .": *Law and Economic Policy,* 85.

p. 18, "The ICC was supposed to . . .": *Pocket History of the United States,* 274–275.

p. 22, "would not submit . . .": *Law and Economic Policy,* 92.

p. 22, "Every contract, combination . . .": *The Antitrust Case Browser,* "The Sherman Antitrust Act (1890), www.stolaf.edu/people/becker/antitrust/statutes/sherman.html (accessed on November 10, 2008).

Chapter 2

p. 25, "In 1885, he became president . . .": "Supreme Court Drama: *Swift and Company* v. *United States,*" Endnotes, www.enotes.com/supreme-court-drama/swift-and-co-v-united-states/print (accessed on November 21, 2008).

p. 27, "There were only eighteen. . .": William Letwin, *Law and Economic Policy in America: The Evolution of the Sherman Antitrust Act* (Chicago: University of Chicago Press, 1981), 103.

p. 28, "the rigid enforcement . . .": *Law and Economic Policy,* p. 117.

p. 29, "incidentally and indirectly . . .": "*United States* v. *E. C. Knight Company,*" *Oyez,* www.oyez.org/cases/1851-1900/1894/1894_675/ (accessed on November 21, 2008).

p. 29, "Riner further stated . . .": *Law and Economic Policy,* 153.

p. 29, "The prohibitory provisions . . .": "*United States* v. *Trans-Missouri Freight Association,*" *Justia,* http://supreme.

justia.com/us/166/290/case.html (accessed on November 16, 2008).

p. 30, "It is no longer . . .": Allan Nevins and Henry Steele Commager, *A Pocket History of the United States* (New York: Pocket Books, 1992), 329.

p. 30, "During the 1890s . . .": Westel Woodbury Willoughby, "Addyston Pipe and Steel Company v. United States," *The Constitutional Law of the United States*, chestofbooks.com/society/law/The-Constitutional-Law-Of-The-United-States/363-Addyston-Pipe-Steel-Co-V-United-States.html (accessed on December 1, 2008).

p. 31, "The Supreme Court's decision . . .": *Law and Economic Policy*, 169.

p. 33, "Judge Taft disagreed . . .": Lester G. Telser, "Genesis of the Sherman Act," University of Chicago, George G. Stigler Center for Study of Economy and State, 1982. www.lib.uchicago.edu/e/busecon/econfac/Telser.html (accessed on November 15, 2008)

p. 34, "The direct and immediate result . . .": "*Addyston Pipe and Steel Company* v. *United States*."

p. 34, "The great corporations . . .": Edmund Morris, *Theodore Rex* (New York: Random House, 2001), 139.

p. 35, "monitor all aspects . . .": *Theodore Rex*, 206.

p. 36, "That is just what . . .": *Theodore Rex*, 91–92.

p. 37, "the constituent companies . . .": "Northern Securities Company v. United States," *Cornell University Law School,* www.law.cornell.edu/supct/html/historics/USSC_CR_0193_0197_ZS.html (accessed on November 16, 2008).

p. 38, "In the case of . . .": "*Swift and Co.* v. *United States*," *Justia,* http://supreme.justia.com/us/196/375/case.html (accessed on January 8, 2009).

Chapter 3

p. 40, "one of the most uncomfortable . . .": "William Howard Taft," *The White House,* www.whitehouse.gov/history/presi dents/wt27.html (accessed on December 1, 2008).

p. 41, "were directed to the suppression . . .": "William How- ard Taft: Inaugural Address," www.bartleby.com/124/pres 43.html (accessed on December 1, 2008).

p. 41, "lawful competitive methods . . .": *Standard Oil Co. of New Jersey* v. *United States,"* *Justia,* http://supreme.justia. com/us/221/1/case.html (accessed on December 1, 2008).

p. 42, "intent and purpose . . .": *"Standard Oil Co. of New Jersey* v. *United States."*

p. 42, "open disregard . . ." "The Rockefellers: People and Events, Ida Tarbell, 1857–1944," *American Experience,* 2000, www.pbs.org/wgbh/amex/rockefellers/peopleevents/p_ tarbell.html (accessed on November 7, 2008).

p. 44, "exercise of judgment . . .": *"Standard Oil Co. of New Jer- sey* v. *United States."*

p. 44, "the standard of reason . . ." *"Standard Oil Co. of New Jersey* v. *United States."*

p. 45, "to control not merely. . .": *"Dr. Miles Medical Co.* v. *John D. Park & Sons Co,"* *FindLaw,* http://caselaw.lp.findlaw.com/ scripts/getcase.pl?court=US&vol=220&invol=373 (accessed on December 1, 2008).

p. 46, "The Clayton Antitrust Act . . .": "The Clayton Antitrust Act (1914)," *The Antitrust Case Browser,* www.stolaf.edu/ people/becker/antitrust/statutes/clayton.html (accessed on December 1, 2008).

p. 48, "business is giving exhibitions . . ." "Federal Baseball Club v. National League," *Justia,* http://supreme.justia.com/ us/259/200/case.html (accessed on December 2, 2008).

p. 49, "it does not follow . . .": Thomas W. Dunfee and Frank F.

Gibson, *Antitrust and Trade Regulation: Cases and Materials* (New York: Wiley, 1985), 63.

Chapter 4

p. 51, "The case involved...": *"Appalachian Coals, Inc. v. United States,"* *Justia,* http://supreme.justia.com/us/288/344/case.html (accessed on December 9, 2008)

p. 53, "have a tendency...": *"Appalachian Coals, Inc. v. United States."*

p. 53, "only a small percentage....": *"Appalachian Coals, Inc. v. United States."*

p. 53, "the essential standard of reasonableness...": *"Appalachian Coals, Inc. v. United States,"* *The Antitrust Case Browser,* www.stolaf.edu/people/becker/antitrust/summaries/288us344.html (accessed on December 9, 2008).

p. 56, "In support of this position . . .": *"Loewe v. Lawlor,"* http://law.jrank.org/pages/13583/Loewe-v-Lawlor.html (accessed on December 10, 2008).

p. 56, "The United Hatters...": *"Lowe v. Lawlor,"*

p. 57, "The labor of human beings . . .": Thomas W. Dunfee and Frank F. Gibson, *Antitrust and Trade Regulation: Cases and Materials* (New York: Wiley, 1985), 245.

p. 60, "As a result of these laws . . .": "Federal Labor Laws," *Congressional Digest,* June–July 1993, www.lectlaw.com/files/emp26.htm (accessed on December 10, 2008).

p. 60, "In 1940, the Supreme Court . . .": *"Apex Hosiery Company v. Leader,"* *FindLaw,* http://caselaw.lp.findlaw.com/cgi-bin/getcase.pl?court=us&vol=310&invol=469 (accessed on December 10, 2008).

p. 60, "Here it is plain . . .": *Apex Hosiery Company v. Leader,"* *FindLaw.*

p. 61, "In the majority opinion...": *"United States v. Hutcheson* et al.," *The Antitrust Case Browser*, www.stolaf.edu/people/becker/antitrust/summaries/312us219.htm (accessed on December 10, 2008).

p. 61, "Author and antitrust lawyer . . .": *Antitrust and Trade Regulation: Cases and Materials*, 240–241.

p. 61, "In addition to labor . . .": Richard Calkins, *Antitrust Guidelines for the Business Executive* (Homewood, IL: Dow Jones-Irwin, 1981), 255–256.

p. 61, "This position was upheld . . .": "*Parker, Director of Agriculture, et al.* v. *Brown,*" *The Antitrust Case Browser*, www.stolaf.edu/people/becker/antitrust/summaries/317us341.html (accessed on December 9, 2008).

p. 62, "In 1936, the Supreme Court . . .": "*International Business Machines Corp.* v. *United States,*" *Justia*, http://supreme.justia.com/us/298/131/case.html (accessed on December 9, 2008).

p. 62, "In the International Salt . . .": "*International Salt Co., Inc.,* v. *United States,*" *Justia*, http://supreme.justia.com/us/332/392/case.html (accessed on December 10, 2008).

p. 64, "In 2007, for example . . .": Andrew Martin, "Wait. Why is the F.T.C. After Whole Foods?" *New York Times*, December 14, 2008, BU 8.

p. 66, "To enhance their business . . .": "*United States* v. *Paramount Pictures, Inc. et al.,*" *The Antitrust Case Browser*, www.stolaf.edu/people/becker/antitrust/summaries/334us131.htm (accessed on December 9, 2008).

Chapter 5

p. 68, "The Yankees decided to keep . . .": Mo Morrissey, "Baseball Labor Relations: Anti-Trust Exemptions and the Reserve Clause," www.associatedcontent.com/pop_print.shtml?content_type=article&content_type_id=421296

(accessed on December 17, 2008).

p. 69, "the business of providing . . .": "*Toolson* v. *New York Yankees*," *Justia*, http://supreme.justia.com/us/346/356/case.html (accessed on December 17, 2008).

p. 69, "Whatever may have been the situation . . .": "*Toolson* v. *New York Yankees.*"

p. 71, "In 1969, St. Louis Cardinal . . .": George Hardin, "Curt Flood Helped Topple Baseball's Reserve Clause," *The Villager*, http://austinvillager.com/sports_060107curtflood.html (accessed on December 17, 2008).

p. 72, "rule established in . . .": "*Radovich* v. *National Football League*," www.stolaf.edu/people/becker/antitrust/summaries/352us445.html (accessed on December 17, 2008).

p. 74, "The phrase 'attempt to monopolize' ": Richard Calkins, *Antitrust Guidelines for the Business Executive* (Homewood, IL: Dow Jones-Irwin, 1981), 153.

p. 74, "This was a case of . . .": *Antitrust Guidelines for the Business Executive*, 84.

p. 76, "did not merely announce . . .": "*United States* v. *Parke, Davis & Co.*," *The Antitrust Case Browser*, www.stolaf.edu/people/becker/antitrust/summaries/362us029.html (accessed on December 16, 2008).

p. 76, "Starting in the 1950s . . .": "*United States* v. *General Motors*," *FindLaw*, http://caselaw.lp.findlaw.com/scripts/getcase.pl?court=US&vol=384&invol=127 (accessed on December 16, 2008).

p. 78, "In one case . . .": Thomas W. Dunfee and Frank F. Gibson, *Antitrust and Trade Regulation: Cases and Materials* (New York: Wiley, 1985), 347-50.

p. 79, "A classic conspiracy . . .": "*United States* v. *General Motors*," *FindLaw*.

p. 79, "Exclusion of traders . . .": *"United States* v. *General Motors," FindLaw.*

p. 79, "elicit from all the dealers . . .": *"United States* v. *General Motors," FindLaw.*

Chapter 6

p. 81, "By 2010, there were . . .": Lee Ann Obringer, "How Franchising Works," *How Stuff Works,* http://money.how stuffworks.com/franchising.htm/printable (accessed on December 20, 2008).

p. 82, "This appeared to violate . . .": Nicholas G. Karambelas, "Franchising in Perspective," *DC Bar,* www.dcbar.org/for_lawyers/resources/publications/washington_lawyer/december (accessed on December 21, 2008).

p. 83, "According to the court documents . . .": *"Susser* v. *Carvel Corp.," AltLaw,* http://altlaw.org/v1/1162834 (accessed on December 21, 2008).

p. 84, "the dealer [franchise owner] . . .": *"Susser* v. *Carvel Corp."*

p. 85, "The fundamental device . . .": *"Susser* v. *Carvel Corp."*

p. 85, "The Siegels claimed . . .": *"Siegel* v. *Chicken Delight," Precydent,* www.precydent.com/citation/448/F.2d/43 (accessed on December 20, 2008).

p. 86, "it is apparent . . .": *"Siegel* v. *Chicken Delight."*

p. 86, "The appeals court also considered . . .": *"Siegel* v. *Chicken Delight."*

p. 86, "The case involved . . .": *"Continental T.V., Inc.* v. *GTE Sylvania Inc.," FindLaw,* http://caselaw.lp.findlaw.com/scripts/getcase.pl?court=US&vol=433&invol=36 (accessed on December 20, 2008).

p. 87, "In 1984, however . . .": Arthur Cantor and Peter Klarfeld, "An Unheralded Stake Through the Heart of *Siegel* v. *Chicken*

Delight and a New Climate for Franchise Tying Claims," *Franchise Law Journal,* Summer 2008, 12.

p. 90, "utterly dependent upon . . .": "*Norman E. Krehl, et al., Plaintiffs,* v. *Baskin-Robbins Ice Cream Company, et al., Defendants,*" *Justia,* http://cases.justia.com/us-court-of-appeals/F2/664/1348/198412/ (accessed on December 20, 2008).

p. 90, "When a manufacturer . . .": *Krehl* v. *Baskin-Robbins.*"

Chapter 7

p. 91, "Group Boycotts, or concerted refusals . . .": Richard Calkins, *Antitrust Guidelines for the Business Executive* (Homewood, IL: Dow Jones-Irwin, 1981), 104. "*United States* v. *General Motors,*" *FindLaw,* http://caselaw.lp.findlaw.com/scripts/getcase.pl?court=US&vol=384&invol=127 (accessed on December 16, 2008).

p. 92, "If Haywood is unable . . ." "*Haywood* v. *National Basketball Assn.,*" *Justia,* http://supreme.justia.com/us/401/1204/case.html (accessed on December 19, 2008).

p. 94, "political message to the public . . .": "*FTC* v. *Superior CT., TLA,*" *Justia,* http://supreme.justia.com/us/493/411/ (accessed on December 28, 2008).

p. 95, "The case involved . . .": "*Northwest Wholesale Stationers, Inc.* v. *Pacific Stationery and Printing Co.,*" *The Association Antitrust Update Website,* 2000, www.gaminggip.com/Cases/FullText/CF-NWStationers.html (accessed on December 18, 2008).

p. 95, "naked restraint of price . . .": "*FTC* v. *Superior CT., TLA,*" *Justia.*

p. 95, "This case involved . . .": "*Summit Health, Ltd.,* v. *Pinhas,*" *Justia,* http://supreme.justia.com/us/500/322/case.html (accessed on December 28, 2008).

p. 97, "the boycott often cut off . . .": "*Northwest Wholesale*

Stationers, Inc. v. *Pacific Stationery and Printing Co."*

p. 98, "A conspiracy to eliminate . . .": *"Summit Health, Ltd.,* v. *Pinhas," Justia.*

p. 99, "For example, suppose four large firms . . .": *Antitrust Guidelines for the Business Executive,* 196–197.

p. 101, "In *Brown Shoe Co. . . .":* *Antitrust Guidelines for the Business Executive,* 201.

p. 101, "the merger spurred . . .": *Antitrust Guidelines for the Business Executive,* 201.

p. 102, "The state sued under . . .": *"California* v. *American Stores,"* FindLaw, http://caselaw.1p.findlaw.com/scripts/getcase.pl?navby=search&court=US&case=/us/495/271.html (accessed on December 26, 2008).

p. 102, "Californians will be irreparably harmed...": *"California* v. *American Stores,"* FindLaw.

p. 102, "In 1997, for example . . .": William F. Shughart, "The Government's War on Mergers," *Cato Institute,* October 1998, 10–12.

p. 103, "In 1974, the Supreme Court . . .": Thomas W. Dunfee and Frank F. Gibson, *Antitrust and Trade Regulation: Cases and Materials* (New York: Wiley, 1985), 206–210.

p. 104, "higher prices and lower quality . . .": "The Government's War on Mergers," 19–20.

Chapter 8

p. 105, "Microsoft was being sued...": Joel Brinkley and Steve Lohr, *U.S.* v. *Microsoft* (New York: McGraw Hill, 2001), 10, 50, 115.

p. 107, "Boies was called an . . .": *U.S.* v. *Microsoft,* 33.

p. 107, "The government's case rested heavily . . .": *U.S.* v. *Microsoft,* 69.

p. 107, "almost from a different era . . .": *U.S.* v. *Microsoft,* 35.

p. 107, "What frightened Microsoft . . .": *U.S. v. Microsoft*, 23.

p. 107, "[We] need a way to push these guys . . .": "U.S. D.C. Circuit Court of Appeals, *USA* v. *Microsoft Corp.*," *FindLaw*, http://laws.findlaw.com/dc/005212a.html (accessed on January 4. 2009).

p. 108, "I do not believe . . .": *U.S. v. Microsoft*, 7–8.

p. 108, "There's a great opportunity....": *U.S. v. Microsoft*, 290.

p. 108, "Instead 'leverage' seemed to mean . . .": "U.S. D.C. Circuit Court of Appeals, *USA* v. *Microsoft Corp.*"

p. 109, "It was clear to us . . .": *U.S. v. Microsoft*, 81.

p. 109, "Gates delivered a . . .": *U.S. v. Microsoft*, 50.

p. 109, " Another way that . . .": *U.S. v. Microsoft*, 8.

p. 109, "During the trial . . .": *U.S. v. Microsoft*, 115.

p. 110, "The company produced evidence . . .": *U.S. v. Microsoft*, 123–24.

p. 110, "Microsoft is constantly . . .": *U.S. v. Microsoft*, 142.

p. 111, "Microsoft maintained its . . .": *U.S. v. Microsoft*, 292, 299–300.

p. 111, "In a decision....": "U.S. D.C. Circuit Court of Appeals, *USA* v. *Microsoft Corp.*"

p. 112, "the most relaxed . . .": Stephen Labaton, "New View of Antitrust Law: See No Evil, Hear No Evil," *New York Times*, May 5, 2006, www.nytimes.com/2006/05/05/business/05legal.html(accessed on January 2, 2009).

p. 113, "Justice Kennedy pointed out . . .": "United States Postal Service v. Flamingo Industries (USA) LTD.," *Justia*, http://supreme.justia.com/us/540/736/case.html (accessed on December 30, 2009).

p. 82, "As Kennedy wrote . . .": "*Leegin Creative Leather Products, Inc.* v. *PSKS, Inc.*, *Justia*, http://supreme.justia.com/us/551/06-480/ (accessed on December 30, 2009).

Further Information

BOOKS

Cefrey, Holly. *The Sherman Antitrust Act: Getting Big Business Under Control*. New York: Rosen, 2004.

Elish, Dan. *Theodore Roosevelt*. New York: Marshall Cavendish Benchmark, 2008.

Lukes, Bonnie. *Woodrow Wilson and the Progressive Era*. Greensboro, NC: Morgan Reynolds, 2006.

Bibliography

BOOKS

Brinkley, Joel, and Steve Lohr. *U.S. v. Microsoft.* New York: McGraw-Hill, 2001.

Calkins, Richard M. *Antitrust Guidelines for the Business Executive.* Homewood, Ill: Dow Jones-Irwin, 1981.

Chernow, Ron. *Titan: The Life of John D. Rockefeller Sr.* New York: Random House, 1998.

Dunfee, Thomas W., and Frank F. Gibson. *Antitrust and Trade Regulation: Cases and Materials.* New York: Wiley, 1985.

Letwin, William. *Law and Economic Policy in America: The Evolution of the Sherman Antitrust Act.* Chicago: University of Chicago Press, 1981.

Morris, Edmund. *Theodore Rex.* New York: Random House, 2001.

Shenefield, John H., and Stelzer, Irwin M. *The Antitrust Laws: A Primer.* Washington, D.C.: The American Enterprise Institute, 1998.

WEBSITES

FindLaw: For Legal Professionals
http://caselaw.lp.findlaw.com
www.findlaw.com/casecode/

Justia: US Supreme Court Center
www.supreme.justia.com

Oyez: U.S. Supreme Court Media
www.oyez.org/cases

All websites were accessible as of October 5, 2010.

Index

Page numbers in **boldface** are illustrations, tables, and charts.

About the Author

RICHARD WORTH is the author of more than fifty books, including books on history, politics, current events, and biographies. His most recent book for Marshall Cavendish Benchmark is *Social Security Act*, in this series. He lives in Connecticut.